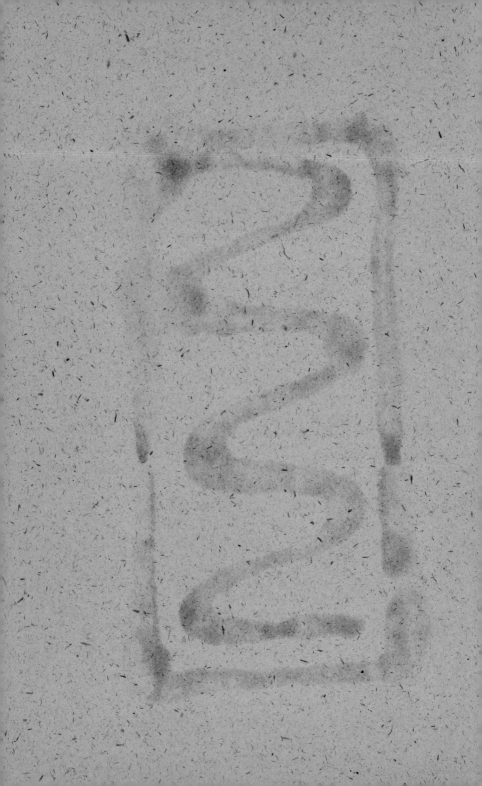

One at a Time

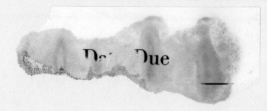

Poems for the Young
by David McCord

Far and Few
Take Sky
All Day Long
Every Time I Climb a Tree†
For Me to Say
Pen, Paper, and Poem
Mr. Bidery's Spidery Garden*
Away and Ago
The Star in the Pail†

* Published in England only
† Illustrated in color by Marc Simont

One at a Time

David McCord

*His collected poems for the young: with full
subject index as well as an index of first lines*

With illustrations by Henry B. Kane

Little, Brown and Company
BOSTON   TORONTO

T 10/77

Second Printing

Library of Congress Cataloging in Publication Data

McCord, David Thompson Watson, 1897-
    One at a time.

    Includes indexes.
    SUMMARY: An illustrated collection of poems about diverse topics including nature, animals, favorite places, and colors.
    [1. American poetry] I. Kane. Henry Bugbee, 1902-1971. II. Title.
PS3525.A1655055   811'.5'2   77-21792
ISBN 0-316-55516-9

Published simultaneously in Canada
by Little, Brown & Company (Canada) Limited

PRINTED IN THE UNITED STATES OF AMERICA

Eleanore Baynton Reed McCord
1863–1956

Wherever she walked, it was morning under the white pine
or beside the sea or on it; and whenever she spoke
or laughed or sang or read aloud, there was
music for a long time. And in her
blue eyes always the blue sky
mending some remembered
day of rain.

Certain of these poems have appeared before in print and I have to thank the following publishers and editors: Charles Scribner's Sons for four poems from *The Crows* by David McCord (copyright 1934, by Charles Scribner's Sons); Doubleday and Company, Inc. for one poem from *A Star by Day* (copyright 1950, by David McCord) and for five lines from *The Camp at Lockjaw* (copyright 1952, by David McCord); Coward-McCann, Inc. for one poem from *And What's More* (copyright 1941, by David McCord); Harcourt, Brace and Company, Inc. for three poems from *Rainbow in the Sky*, edited by Louis Untermeyer (copyright 1935 by Harcourt, Brace and Company, Inc.); *The Saturday Review of Literature; The New Yorker* (the poem "Cocoon" was copyrighted in 1949 by The New Yorker Magazine, Inc., under the title of "Sing Cocoon"); *Ladies' Home Journal; The Atlantic Monthly; The Boston Globe; Harvard Alumni Bulletin; The Horn Book; New York Times Book Review; Boston Magazine; Cricket; Yankee;* A and A Distributors, Inc. "The Tree" (with an illustration by Chiang Yee) was printed as a Christmas poem by Harold Hugo and the Meriden Gravure Company in 1965. "To a Child" is reprinted from *The Crows*, copyright 1934 by Charles Scribner's Sons; copyright renewed in 1962 by David McCord. "How to Draw a Monkey" is reprinted by permission from the January 1969 issue of *Good Housekeeping*, copyright © 1969 by the Hearst Corporation. The poems in the section "Write Me Another Verse" appeared in David McCord's book *Pen, Paper, and Poem* published by Holt, Rinehart and Winston, Inc. The selection is included in this book by permission of the publisher. "Mr. Bidery's Spidery Garden" was originally included in Louis Untermeyer's *Fun and Nonsense*, a Giant Golden Book, copyright © 1970 by Western Publishing Company, Inc.

Introduction

All the poems in this book were written one at a time. Not, of course, according to any fixed schedule as to what each poem would be about or when it would be written, or how long it would take to write it. People who work in an office, factory, laboratory, school, hospital; or on a farm, on board a ship, plane, or train, have certain regular duties to perform. They know perfectly well, even before breakfast, what these duties are like. Likewise a painter, sculptor, or composer of music, I think—though I may be wrong—has a fairly positive plan for the work ahead from day to day.

But the poet—what is he? Why, he is more like the fireman waiting for a fire; the ambulance driver waiting for an accident, an illness, or a tragedy; a policeman in his cruise car waiting for a call over the intercom for immediate and possibly dangerous action.

But you must understand that here I am talking solely about the poet concerned with poems at least in some respect like those in this book: most of them relatively short. Once he has the idea for a poem he will also have, if he is any good at all, an immediate urge to write it. This may happen anytime, any place, day or night, on land or sea or in the air. The better and more exciting the idea, the sooner the poem will be written. The first draft of it will be written rather rapidly, in a matter of minutes or hours, though the final tinkering with rhyme and accent, the desperate search for the right word in a difficult line, may stretch into days, even alas! into weeks. Only on rare occasions does an idea for a poem have to be stored away in the mind for months or possibly for years before the writer (I, in any case) can put pen to paper. Of course the great poet, endlessly struggling over some *Paradise Lost*, may take time out now and then to fool with a sonnet or something rather brief. Robert Frost once told me that he wrote "Stopping by Woods on a Snowy Evening"—one of his most famous poems—the very night he was so busy with the much longer poem called "New Hampshire." Not many fifth graders today, I would guess, have read "New Hampshire"; but I know through experience that thousands of fifth graders, let alone fourth, sixth, seventh, and eighth graders, know "Stopping by Woods" by heart. Frost died in 1963; but lots of children knew that poem when he was alive. When I was young, all poets were supposed to be dead.

Well, this book that you have opened contains, with a single exception, all of my poems first published in *Far and Few, Take Sky, All Day Long, For Me to Say,* and *Away and Ago.* If not one of them seems familiar to you, I suggest that you look at any two or three of the following: "Every Time I Climb a Tree," "The Pickety Fence," "Take Sky," "Three Signs of Spring," "Scat! Scitten!," "Fast and Slow," "Rapid Reading," "Sunfish," "The Game of Doublets," "The Importance of Eggs," "The Walnut Tree," "The Star in the Pail," "Runover Rhyme," "Write Me a Verse," "Little," and "The Cellar Hole." And if you are particularly interested in birds or animals; bugs, bats, fish, frogs; ducks, geese, and chickens; or nonsense verse; or sounds or colors; rain, snow, and wind, look them up in the subject index at the back of the book.

Henry B. Kane, an old friend, a fine naturalist, writer, photographer, and artist, whose drawings add so much to these poems, for whatever they are worth, died a few days after he had finished illustrating *For Me to Say* back in

1970. He is at his tremendous best, it seems to me, in such pictures as the ants, 306; bird's nest, 351; crow, 94; frogs, 274, 386; mobile, 254; owl, 228; pumpkins, 286; skunk cabbage, 246; snapping turtle, 317; steam engine— a carefully drawn reminder of the most exciting and visibly splendid machine ever made, because you could *see* almost all of its working parts in action—106; toad, 80; lone surviving turkey—very *very* sad, 236.

In homage to Henry B. Kane, the publishers and I have limited the drawings in this book to his alone.

Blesséd Lord, what it is to be young:
To be of, to be for, be among—
Be enchanted, enthralled,
Be the caller, the called,
The singer, the song, and the sung.

D. T. W. McC.

Contents

One at a Time

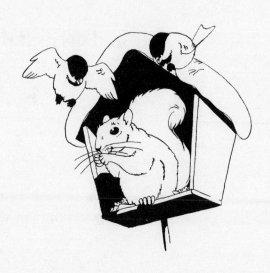

Joe

We feed the birds in winter,
And outside in the snow
We have a tray of many seeds
For many birds of many breeds
And one gray squirrel named Joe.
    But Joe comes early,
    Joe comes late,
    And all the birds
    Must stand and wait.
And waiting there for Joe to go
Is pretty cold work in the snow.

3

Five Little Bats

Five little bats flew out of the attic:
Five little bats all acrobatic.

One little bat flew through the city,
One little bat was flitting pretty.

One little bat flew round the gable,
One little bat was not flight able.

One little bat flew in and out of
Something or other, I haven't a doubt of

That, or that five little bats erratic
Flew back in and are now up attic.

Five Chants

1

Every time I climb a tree
Every time I climb a tree
Every time I climb a tree
I scrape a leg
Or skin a knee
And every time I climb a tree
I find some ants
Or dodge a bee
And get the ants
All over me

And every time I climb a tree
Where have you been?
They say to me
But don't they know that I am free
Every time I climb a tree?
I like it best
To spot a nest
That has an egg
or maybe three

5

And then I skin
The other leg
But every time I climb a tree
I see a lot of things to see
Swallows rooftops and TV
And all the fields and farms there be
Every time I climb a tree
Though climbing may be good for ants
It isn't awfully good for pants
But still it's pretty good for me
Every time I climb a tree

II

Monday morning back to school
Fool fool fool fool
Monday morning back we go
No No No No
Monday morning summer's gone
John John John John
Monday morning what a pain
Jane Jane Jane Jane

III

The pickety fence
The pickety fence
Give it a lick it's
The pickety fence
Give it a lick it's
A clickety fence
Give it a lick it's
A lickety fence
Give it a lick
Give it a lick
Give it a lick
With a rickety stick
Pickety
Pickety
Pickety
Pick

IV

The cow has a cud
The turtle has mud
The rabbit has a hutch
But I haven't much

The ox has a yoke
The frog has a croak
The toad has a wart
So he's not my sort

The mouse has a hole
The polecat a pole
The goose has a hiss
And it goes like this

The duck has a pond
The bird has beyond
The hen has a chick
But I feel sick

The horse has hay
The dog has his day
The bee has a sting
And a queen not a king

The robin has a worm
The worm has a squirm
The squirrel has a nut
Every wheel has a rut

The pig has a pen
The bear has a den
The trout has a pool
While I have school

The crow has a nest
The hawk has a quest
The owl has a mate
Doggone! I'm late!

V

Thin ice
Free advice
Heavy snow
Out you go
Nice slush
Lush lush
Wet feet
Fever heat
Stuffy head
Stay in bed
Who's ill?
Me? A pill?

The Rainbow

The rainbow arches in the sky,
But in the earth it ends;
And if you ask the reason why,
They'll tell you "That depends."

It never comes without the rain,
Nor goes without the sun;
And though you try with might and main,
You'll never catch me one.

Perhaps you'll see it once a year,
Perhaps you'll say: "No, twice";
But every time it does appear,
It's very clean and nice.

If I were God, I'd like to win
At sun-and-moon croquet:
I'd drive the rainbow-wickets in
And ask someone to play.

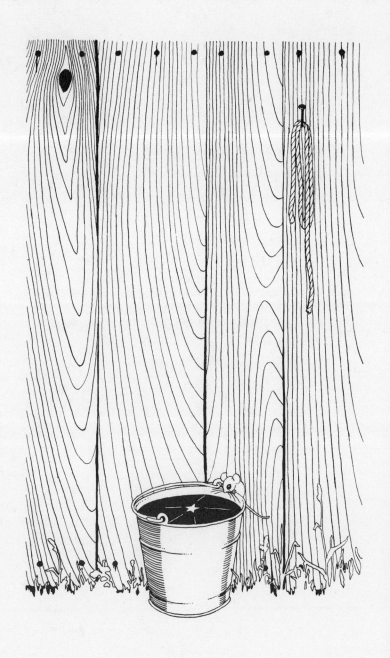

12

The Star in the Pail

I took the pail for water when the sun was high
And left it in the shadow of the barn nearby.

When evening slippered over like the moth's brown wing,
I went to fetch the water from the cool wellspring.

The night was clear and warm and wide, and I alone
Was walking by the light of stars as thickly sown

As wheat across the prairie, or the first fall flakes,
Or spray upon the lawn — the kind the sprinkler makes.

But every star was far away as far can be,
With all the starry silence sliding over me.

And every time I stopped I set the pail down slow,
For when I stooped to pick the handle up to go

Of all the stars in heaven there was one to spare,
And he silvered in the water and I left him there.

At the Garden Gate

Who so late
At the garden gate?
Emily, Kate,
And John.
"John,
Where have you been?
It's after six;
Supper is on,
And you've been gone
An hour,
John!"
"We've been, we've been,
We've just been over
The field," said
John.
(Emily, Kate,
And John.)

Who so late
At the garden gate?
Emily, Kate,
And John.
"John,
What have you got?"
"A whopping toad.
Isn't he big?

14

He's a terrible
Load.
(We found him
A little ways
Up the road,"
Said Emily,
Kate,
And John.)

Who so late
At the garden gate?
Emily, Kate,
And John.
"John,
Put that thing down!
Do you want to get warts?"
(They all three have 'em
By last
Reports.)
Still, finding toads
Is the best of
Sports,
Say Emily,
Kate,
And John.

The Fisherman

The little boy is fishing
With a green fishline,
And he has got me wishing
That his line were mine.

The little boy is fishing
With a fresh-cut pole,
And he has got me wishing
For his fishing hole.

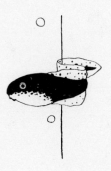

The little boy is fishing
With better than a pin,
And he has got me wishing
That he won't fall in.

The little boy is fishing
With a disenchanted slug,
And he has got me wishing
For the first faint tug.

The little boy is fishing
With a cider-cork float,
And he has got me wishing
For the cider and a boat.

The little boy is fishing
For I don't know what,
And he has got my wishing
In an awful knot.

Something Better

We have a nice clean new green lawn,
And that's the one I'm playing on.
But down the street a little piece
There is a man who has three geese.
And when you see them, just beyond
You'll see a nice new deep blue pond.

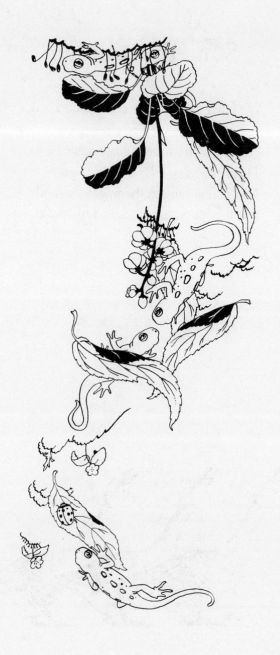

The Newt

The little newt
Is not a brute,
A fish or fowl,
A kind of owl:
He doesn't prowl
Or run or dig
Or grow too big.
He doesn't fly
Or laugh or cry —
He doesn't try.

The little newt
Is mostly mute,
And grave and wise,
And has two eyes.
He lives inside,
Or likes to hide;
But after rain
He's out again
And rather red,
I should have said.

The little newt
Of great repute
Has legs, a tail,
A spotted veil.

He walks alone
From stone to stone,
From log to log,
From bog to bog,
From tree to tree,
From you to me.

The little newt
By grass or root
Is very kind
But hard to find.
His hands and feet
Are always neat:
They move across
The mildest moss.
He's very shy,
He's never spry —
Don't ask me why.

Tim

When Tim was six or seven or eight —
not five or four or three,
he learned a lot of things: to skate,
to climb a white birch tree;
to imitate a frog, fly kites,
or even go to sea
in farmer's pond, about as wide
as eight bathtubs would be —
about as deep as any cow
could wish: up to her knee.
That's how it was at six or seven
or eight, not five-four-three.

Some other things Tim learned, was how
to multiply by nine,
beware of bees around a hive,
to leave a porcupine
alone; and recognize the leaves
of that wild sneaky vine
called poison ivy; *really* test
a last-year's fishing line
to see that it won't break; and take
some pride in making fine
clear letters when he wrote;
to know five needles mean white pine.

Father and I in the Woods

"Son,"
My father used to say,
"Don't run."

"Walk,"
My father used to say,
"Don't talk."

"Words,"
My father used to say,
"Scare birds."

So be:
It's sky and brook and bird
And tree.

Dividing

Here is an apple, ripe and red
   On one side; on the other green.
And I must cut it with a knife
   Across or in between.

And if I cut it in between,
   And give the best (as Mother said)
To you, then I must keep the green,
   And you will have the red.

But Mother says that green is tough
   Unless it comes in applesauce.
You *know* what? I've been sick enough:
   I'll cut it straight across.

The Frost Pane

What's the good of breathing
On the window
Pane
In summer?
You can't make a frost
On the window pane
In summer.
You can't write a
Nalphabet,
You can't draw a
Nelephant;

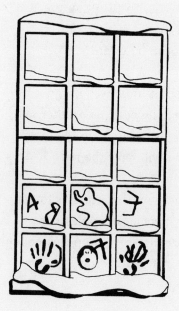

You can't make a smudge
With your nose
In summer.

Lots of good, breathing
On the window
Pane
In winter.
You can make a frost
On the window pane
In winter.
A white frost, a light frost,
A thick frost, a quick frost,
A write-me-out-a-picture frost
Across the pane
In winter.

The Grasshopper

Down
a
deep
well
a
grasshopper
fell.

By kicking about
He thought to get out.
      He might have known better,
      For that got him wetter.
To kick round and round
Is the way to get drowned,
      And drowning is what
      I should tell you he got.

But
the
well
had
a
rope
that
dangled
some
hope.

And sure as molasses
On one of his passes
   He found the rope handy
   And up he went, *and he*

it
up
and
it
up
and
it
up
and
it
up
went

And hopped away proper
As any grasshopper.

The Hunter

The tiny young hunter arose with the morn.
He took up his gun and his powder horn,
And hied him away for the fields of the sun
With his wee powder horn and his minikin gun.

The tiny young hunter looked into the wood
That frowned on the fields of the sun where he stood;
He shot him a fox and a rabbit and one
Silinikin bear with his minikin gun.

Far, far from his wood by the fields of the sun,
With his wee powder horn and his minikin gun,
The tiny young hunter returned to his bed
And dreamed he went hunting again (so he said).

Tiger Lily

The tiger lily is a panther,
Orange to black spot:
Her tongue is the velvet pretty anther,
And she's in the vacant lot.

The cool day lilies grow beside her,
But they are done now and dead,
And between them a little silver spider
Hangs from a thread.

The Firetender

Each morning when the dawn returns,
And hills and trees and fields and ferns
Are grateful in the gaining light,
He rises from the dead of night
And rakes the star-coals up the sky
Until the flames burn bright and high,
And every cloud that eastward is
Is reddened by that fire of his.

At evening when the day is done,
And comes an end of play and fun,
The old Firetender lifts his rake —
He gives the sky a mighty shake,
And down the west the star-coals roll,
To scatter in the western bowl.
He watches the reflection spread,
Then banks the fire and goes to bed.

Notice

I have a dog,
I had a cat.
I've got a frog
Inside my hat.

Rhyme

The bee thrives
on honey and hives,
the cat apparently
has nine lives,
Bluebeard was difficult
for wives,
and someday I shall count
by fives.

Tick-Tock Talk

Big clocks go *tick,*
Big clocks go *tock.*
The ticking always seems to mock

The tocking. Don't the tocks sound thick
Compared with ticks, whose tongues are quick?

"The clock is *ticking,*" people say.
No clocks are ever *tocking.* They

Make just as many tocks as ticks!
It's sad to see tocks in a fix

Like this: I'd love to know some clocks
That have no ticks at all — just tocks.

One thing you'll notice, though, is when
Clocks strike the hour — five or ten,

Or two or six, say; twelve or three —
They're telling you what they tell me

About the tick-tocks: something's *wrong,*
The sour way that clocks go *Bong!*

Yellow

Green is go,
and red is stop,
and yellow is peaches
with cream on top.

Earth is brown,
and blue is sky;
yellow looks well
on a butterfly.

Clouds are white,
black, pink, or mocha;
yellow's a dish of
tapioca.

The Door

Why is there more
behind a door
than there is
before:
kings,
things
in store:
faces,
places
to explore:
The marvelous shore,
the rolling floor,
the green man
by the sycamore?

This Is My Rock

This is my rock,
And here I run
To steal the secret of the sun;

This is my rock,
And here come I
Before the night has swept the sky;

This is my rock,
This is the place
I meet the evening face to face.

Tiggady Rue

Curious, curious Tiggady Rue
Looks and looks in the heart of you;
She finds you good,
She finds you bad,
Generous, mean,
Grumpy, glad —
Tiggady Rue.

Curious, curious Tiggady Rue
Tells your thoughts and tells you *you;*
Elephant thoughts,
And spry and lean,
And thoughts made like a jumping bean,
Or wedgy ones
Slid in between —
She knows them, too,
If she looks at you,
Tiggady Rue.

Curious, curious Tiggady Rue
Knows your thoughts and you and you.
When dusk is down
On field and town,
Beware!
Take care!
If she looks at you —
Tiggady Rue.

Earth Song

Let me dry you, says the desert;
Let me wet you, says the sea.
If that's the way they talk, why don't
They talk that way to me?

Let me fan you, says the wind;
Oh, let me cool you, says the rain.
Let me bury you, the snow says;
Let me dye you with the stain

Of sunset, says the evening;
Let me float you, says the lake;
Let me drift you, says the river.
Says the temblor, let me shake

You. *Freeze* you, says the glacier;
Let me burn you, says the sun.
I don't know what the moon says,
Or that star — the green pale one.

Question

Who says, But one month more
and the days grow shorter?
Some gloomy Gus, I guess,
some wretched roving reporter —
of mine no kith or kin.
Don't let him in.

Who says, But one month more
and the days grow longer?
Don't know. I couldn't guess.
His appeal, though, is stronger.
He doesn't frown? He has a grin?
He *has?* Oh, let him in!

All About Fireflies All About

The stars are all so far away
For creature-kind that hide by day
(For moth and mouse and toad and such)
The starlight doesn't count for much.
And that is why a field at night
In May or June is plaintive, bright
With little lanterns sailing by,
Like stars across a mimic sky,
Just high enough — but not too high.

46

Compass Song

North, south, east, and west,
Summer, spring, winter, fall:
Each of you I love the best,
All of you — *all.*

Summernorth, wintersouth,
Eastfall and westspring:
Clapper in the big bell mouth,
Ring the bell — *ring!*

From the Mailboat Passing By

In the long lake's mirror
Everything is upside down.
But nothing could be clearer:
Mountain, bridge, and town;
    Pine tree, birch, and oak,
      Tall smoke,
    All topside upside down:
      Even the fisherfolk,
      Even a smile or frown.

Tomorrows

Tomorrows never seem to stay,
Tomorrow will be yesterday
Before you know.
Tomorrows have a sorry way
Of turning into just today,
And so . . . and so . . .

Alarm

"There's a cat out there."
"Cat? How do you know?"
"I hear the robins saying so."

"There's a hawk somewhere."
"Don't see a hawk."
"The chickens do. Hear the hens' hawk-squawk?
The young chicks heard it. They've run for cover.
A hawk need only fly, not hover.
See how one hen has cocked an eye?
That's not a crow just flying by.
Hens know *his* flight. Might be an owl;
Except the short-eared one: he's rare.
If you're like me, you don't much care
For jays; but though the jay is all
For robbing birds' nests, his loud call
At any sign of danger wakes
The world around him: cats, black snakes,
Shrikes, hawks, dogs, weasels, squirrels, crows, rats!

But robins specialize on cats."

In the Middle

I think about the elephant and flea,
For somewhere in between them there is me.

Perhaps the flea is unaware of this:
Perhaps I'm not what elephants would miss.

I don't know how the flea puts in his day;
I guess an elephant just likes to sway.

But there they are: one little and one large,
And in between them only me in charge!

Mr. Macklin's Jack o'Lantern

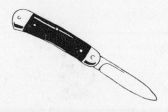

Mr. Macklin takes his knife
And carves the yellow pumpkin face:
Three holes bring eyes and nose to life,
The mouth has thirteen teeth in place.

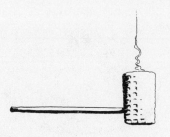

Then Mr. Macklin just for fun
Transfers the corncob pipe from his
Wry mouth to Jack's, and everyone
Dies laughing! O what fun it is

Till Mr. Macklin draws the shade
And lights the candle in Jack's skull.
Then all the inside dark is made
As spooky and as horrorful

As Halloween, and creepy crawl
The shadows on the toolhouse floor,
With Jack's face dancing on the wall.
O Mr. Macklin! Where's the door?

Snail

This sticky trail
Was made by snail.
Snail makes no track
That he'll take back.
However slow,
His word is go.
(Twixt me and you
The word is goo.)

That's Not

That's not a grouse — a pheasant;
rather tame. The male's unpleasant
voice is telling you, "I'm present!"

That's not a raven, not a rook.
A crow dislikes to be mistook
for either! Take a careful look.

That's *not* a wildcat. That's a lynx.
Mistake a weasel for a mink's
a sign you don't know speed, methinks.

No rabbit *that*. No, sir! a *hare:*
long ears, long legs. But not long where
you're looking. Please learn not to stare.

The Starfish

When I see a starfish
Upon the shining sand,
I ask him how he liked the sea
And if he likes the land.
"Would you rather be a starfish
Or an out-beyond-the-bar fish?"
I whisper very softly,
And he seems to understand.

He never *says* directly,
But I fancy all the same
That he knows the answer quite as well
As if it were his name:
"An out-beyond-the-bar fish
Is much happier than a starfish";
And when I look for him again
He's gone the way he came.

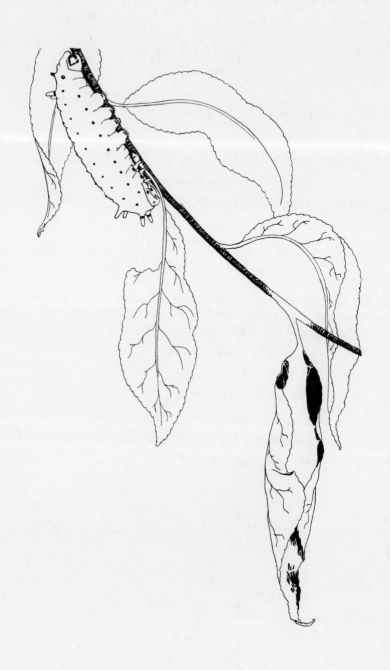

Cocoon

The little caterpillar creeps
Awhile before in silk it sleeps.
It sleeps awhile before it flies,
And flies awhile before it dies,
And that's the end of three good tries.

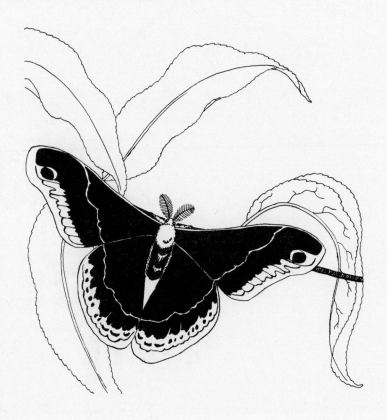

Waltzing Mice

Every night as I go to bed
I think of the prayer I should have said;
And even now as I bow my head:
"Please, O Lord, may I have instead
Some waltzing mice, a gun, and a sled?"

I don't suppose they're much of a price,
But Uncle Ted (without advice)
Gave me skates, and there isn't ice;
And I could have been saying, "How terribly *nice*,
A gun, a sled, and waltzing mice!"

Every night when play is done,
I think them all over, one by one;
"And quite the splendidest, Lord, for fun
Are waltzing mice, a sled, and a gun."

Smart Mr. Doppler

Smart Mr. Doppler
Was a queer sort of bird,
Not for things he did
But for sounds he heard.
Well, the sounds he heard
Are the sounds we hear,
But this Mr. Doppler
Had the better ear,
And this Mr. Doppler
Had the brighter mind;
So today one sound is the Doppler kind.

Hearing all the clamor
Of an engine bell,
He knew that it was coming
If it seemed to swell:
clang CLANG CLANG CLANG CLANG!
          (it rang)
CLANG CLANG CLANG CLANG *clang*.

And that was another very odd thing too:
The pitch went down when the sound passed through:
        clang
        CLANG
        CLANG
        CLANG
        CLANG!

(past you)
CLANG
CLANG
CLANG
CLANG
clang.

Smart Mr. Doppler
Is long since gone:
But you can hear him everywhere
From dark to dawn.
From dawn to dark
You can hear him:
                    HARK!

Riding on the train
When another goes by,
With the bell ding . . . *dong* . . . ding . . .
higher, HIGHER, HIGH;
With the ding-dong-dang of it,
LOWER, LOWER, *low*. . . .

When you hear it so
You will always know
That smart Mr. Doppler
Is still on the go!

Owls Talking

I think that many owls say *Who-o:*
At least the owls that I know do-o.
But somewhere when some owls do not-t,
Perhaps they cry *Which-h, Why-y, or What-t.*

Or when they itch-h
They just say *Which-h,*
Or close one eye-e
And try *What-t Why-y.*

Far Away

How far, today,
Is far away?
It's farther now than I can say,
It's farther now than you can say,
It's farther now than who can say,
It's very *very* far away:
You'd better better better play,
You'd better stay and play today.
Okay . . . okay . . . okay.

Centipede

This centipede has fifty legs
and fifty others which are pegs.
The tragedy occurred on ice:
he slipped, lost fifty in a trice.
And since no trace of trice was found,
he barely managed on the ground
with half his legs not under him;
but could no longer on a limb
have fifty back legs firmly there
against the bark, as in the air
he'd wave the other fifty. You've
seen how he does it. You approve
of fifty peg legs for this chap?
Some people wouldn't give a rap.

Easter Morning: *Three Poems*

Question: What kind of rabbit can an Easter rabbit be?
What is the rabbit's habitat? A regular rabbitry?
We pause ten minutes now, while I consider this.
    Let's see.

In the first place, have you evidence that Easter
    rabbits *do*
Exist? You have? Who else would hide, you say, those
    eggs for you?
Who else indeed! Good point! But do they have a
    working crew?

That is: What makes you *think* those special rabbits
    are a breed?
Take Santa Claus. It seems that only one is all we need.
Why not *one* Easter rabbit, then? He's surely got
    more speed

Than Santa. And he likewise has no chimney
    problems. No,
He doesn't have a hole, of course, for he doesn't have
    to go
To the Duchess's tea party. And he has no
    Christmas flow

Of letters, asking for this and that: eggs are all you get.
The best that I can think of is, that since we've
     never met
This Easter rabbit, keep on trying. You just may meet
     him yet.

2

Mr. Rabbit, a basket on his arm,
Meets Mrs. Hen, quite busy on the farm.
"You've got some eggs saved up for me?"
Mrs. Hen says, "Yes. I've saved you three.
Right back of the nest. You'll find them there."
"Mrs. Duck? Think she's got some to spare?"
"You'll have to ask her. She's on the pond.
I don't think many kids are fond
Of duck eggs, though." "A special taste,"
Says Mr. Rabbit. "But I can't waste
This Easter morning, alas, alas!
Okay. I'll let the duck eggs pass.
I have five others — hens' eggs, you know.
But I must color them so they'll show
Up when the kids start hunting for 'em.
Eight eggs on Easter Day's a quorum —
If you know what a quorum is."
"I don't," says Mrs. Hen. "My biz
Is laying eggs. I've got the habit,

But not for *you!* Why should a rabbit
Go round with baskets full of what
He'll hide? For *I* know that they're not
All found." "I boil 'em, Mrs. Hen."
"Well, go and get them boiling then!"

    3

Is Easter just a day of hats,
Of Easter eggs from Bunny?
Is church on Easter something that's
Tomorrow if it's sunny?

You know the date: first Sunday — well?
"To follow the first full moon . . ."
"That follows the Vernal Equi — tell
Me!" . . . "nox!" That's pretty soon:

March 21. Oh, Easter means
The goddess of the spring
Who supervised the gardens, greens,
Birds, flowers, everything.

But Easter, oh, it means much more:
Christ risen from the dead;
His spirit in the heart before
We lose it in the head;

The resurrection of our love,
Compassion — sharing joy
In gratitude that we are of
This world: a girl, a boy.

The Shell

I took away the ocean once,
Spiraled in a shell,
And happily for months and months
I heard it very well.

How is it then that I should hear
What months and months before
Had blown upon me sad and clear,
Down by the grainy shore?

Watching the Moon

September evenings such as these
The moon hides early in the trees,
And when we drive along the shore
I think I miss the trees the more
Because the moon is coming down
Beyond the branches and will drown.

Pome

Hlo
Outen myuncles varmule see
a nash a noak anna napple tree
an est three yeggs anna nold why ten
six sources scows buy a bigpigpen
pig skitten sand one colleap up
with lots ford inner yumyum sup
goobye

Asleep and Awake

Nothing in the sky is high,
Nothing in the sea is deep,
Nothing on the street goes by
When I'm asleep.

Nothing but the world is wide,
Nothing but a storm can break,
Nothing but a star can hide
When I'm awake.

The White Ships

Out from the beach the ships I see
On cloudy sails move sleepily,
And though the wind be fair and strong
I watch them steal like ants along,
Following free, or wheeling now
To dip the sun a golden prow.

But when I ride upon the train
And turn to find the ships again,
I catch them far against the sky,
With crowded canvas hurrying by,
To all intent as fast as we
Are thundering beside the sea.

At Low Tide

A broken saucer of the sea
Is lying on the sand,
With seaweed like the leaves of tea,
Brown as the boy's brown hand —

The small brown boy with pail and spade,
The connoisseur of kelp,
Considering what the tide has made
And best how he can help.

The Wind

Wind in the garden,
Wind on the hill,
Wind I-am-blowing,
Never be still.

Wind I-am-blowing,
I love you the best:
Out of the morning,
Into the west.

Out of the morning,
Washed in the blue,
Wind I-am-blowing,
Where are you?

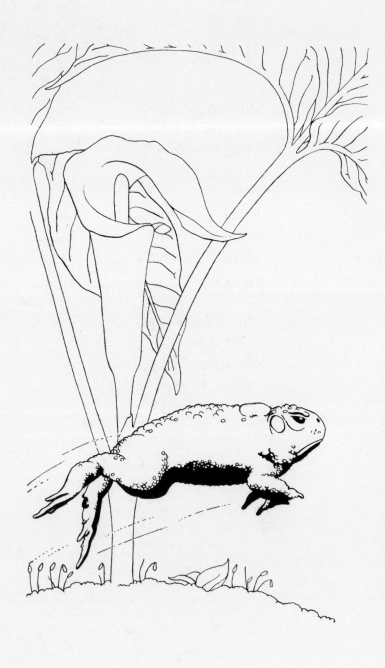

Our Mr. Toad

Our Mr. Toad
Has a nice abode
Under the first front step.
When it rains he's cool
In a secret pool
Where the water goes
    drip
    drop
    drep.

Our Mr. Toad
Will avoid the road:
He's a private-cellar man.
And it's not much fun
In the broiling sun
When you *have* a good
    ten
    tone
    tan.

Our Mr. Toad
Has a kind of code
That tells him the coast is clear.
Then away he'll hop
With a stop, stop, stop
When the dusk draws
    nigh
    no
    near.

Fat Father Robin

Fat father robin,
A red rubber ball,
Rolls across the lawn
And bounces off the wall.

Rolls, bounces, rolls away,
Hearing in the ground
The worm talking tunnel
And the mole saying mound.

August 28

A flock of swallows have gone flying south;
The bluejay carries acorns in his mouth.
I don't know where he carries them or why.
I'm never sure I like the bluejay's cry,
But still I like his blue shape in the sky.

John

John comes in with a basket:
John is a neighborly man.
I have a question — I ask it:
John, can I mix the bran
And make the mash
With a splash in the pan
And feed the pig —
Not the awfully big
One — the little one? Can
I, John?

John comes in with a basket:
The basket is full of wood.
I have a question — I ask it:
John, if I'm awfully good,
Could I help today
With the hay? If I should,

I'd like to rake
While the others make.
I'd be good. Now could
I, John?

John comes in with a basket:
The basket is full of flowers.
I have a question — I ask it:
John, if it rains or showers
How would it seem
To your team of plowers
To follow for worms
With attracting squirms
And fish for hours,
Hey, John?

John comes in with a basket:
The basket is full of fruit.
I have a question — I ask it:
John, would you like to shoot
With the Indian bow

Of a Crow or a Ute —
And arrows too,
If we find a few?
We could look. Would it suit
You, John?

John comes in with a basket:
The basket is full of peas.
I have a question — I ask it:
John, if it blows a breeze,
Why couldn't we — well,
If I shelled all these —
Go fly my kite
To a flyable height
Where there aren't any trees,
Eh, John?

John comes in with a basket:
The basket that has no lid.

I have a question — I ask it:
John, there's a hen that's hid
Her nest in the loft
Where I've often slid,
But I've messed it some.
Do you think she'll come
To sit where she did
Sit, John?

John comes in with a basket:
A basket that's empty, too.
I have a question — I ask it:
John, did you know I knew?
Tomorrow we'll pack
And go back. It's true.
Do you mind to stay
With the snow and the sleigh?
I'll miss you. Will you
Me, John?

Lost

I have a little turtle
Name of Myrtle.
I have an extra lizard
Name of Wizard.
I have two kinds of snake:
Bill and Blake.
I have a dandy hutch
Without the rabbit.
If you see any such,
Will you please grab it?

Sunfish

The sunfish, funny finny one,
is plainly unconcerned with sun;
he is, though, on the other hand,
concerned about the boy on land,
who floats a cork from which depends —
hangs down; or, if you will, descends —
into the quiet of the pool
a string or line. To that the fool
has tied a leader made of gut.
Fish aren't supposed to see it, but
they do; what's more, they see the hook
attached, and take a second look —
perhaps a third, fourth, fifth. Look six
is for the barby part that pricks.
Still, not by hooks are fish allured,
but by the smell of sugar-cured
Virginia ham, to speak in terms
of what *we'd* bite. The fish bite worms.
And half a worm, perhaps the whole
of one, is acting in the role
of tempter.
          Where's that sunfish? Here
he is; and swimming rather queer,
because he had a worm in mind.

Today the bait is bacon rind.
Now what sunfish who isn't blind
has ever seen sliced bacon rind?
The lean part — yes, perhaps the fat —
in strips looks like a worm; but that
it *doesn't* squirm has got the poor
sunfish examining this lure.
Then, too, the shadow of the rod
where no branch was seems *very* odd!
The boy himself sits on the bank
to feel the tug and give the yank.
But he is partly out of sight.

Let's wait for that sunfish to bite.
On second thought, let's not. All right?

Durenda Fair

Shapely, sharp Durenda Fair
Wore three roses in her hair:
One for love and one for grace
And one for any time and place.

Crows

I like to walk
And hear the black crows talk.

I like to lie
And watch crows sail the sky.

I like the crow
That wants the wind to blow:

I like the one
That thinks the wind is fun.

I like to see
Crows spilling from a tree,

And try to find
The top crow left behind.

I like to hear
Crows caw that spring is near.

I like the great
Wild clamor of crow hate

Three farms away
When owls are out by day.

I like the slow
Tired homeward-flying crow;

I like the sight
Of crows for my good night.

Yellow Jacket

A yellow jacket scares me;
hornets never do or did.
A hornet's nest prepares me
by its size — it won't stay hid.

The yellow jacket's nest is
in the ground, so I believe;
but rarely where that pest is
seen to enter or to leave!

Once picking berries, blue ones,
in the shale the Poconos
are noted for — the true ones
grow in Maine, as you-all knows.

(I don't see where I get that
you-all stuff, unheard in Maine.)
Where was I? Oh, yes! Not that
it much matters now. The pain

in my right ankle's easing.
Thanks! It's quite a while ago
that I was out that pleasing
berry day in Pocono.

Two yellow jackets must have
been quite close and on the ground.
I couldn't say. I just have
no idea. There was no sound.

They stung me, though. And yelling —
did I say I was alone?
Of course! That's why I'm telling
you all this. The anklebone,

when stung, produces curious
reactions in the child;
the yellow jackets furious.
I'd probably defiled

their nest I didn't search for:
seemed no reason to stand by.
I left them in the lurch for
good. You like blueberry pie?

Who Wants a Birthday?

Who wants a birthday?
Somebody does.

"I *am*," says a birthday,
But never "I *was*."

"Five, six," says a birthday:
"You're seven!" "You're nine!"

"I'm yours," says a birthday,
"And you, child, are mine."

"*How* old?" says a birthday.
(You have to guess right.)

"You're *what?*" says a birthday.
(You may be: you *might*.)

"A cake," says a birthday,
"I'm sure there's a cake!"

"A wish," says a birthday.
"What wish do you make?"

"I'm glad," says a birthday,
"To see how you've grown."

"Hello!" says a birthday.
("Hello!" says my own.)

Isabel Jones & Curabel Lee

Isabel Jones & Curabel Lee
Lived on butter and bread and tea,
And as to that they would both agree:
Isabel, Curabel, Jones & Lee.

Isabel said: While prunes have stones
They aren't a promising food for Jones;
Curabel said: Well, as for me,
Tripe is a terrible thing for Lee.

There's not a dish of fowl or fish
For which we wish, said I. & C.
And that is why until we die
We'll eat no pie, nor beg nor buy
But butter and bread and a trace of tea.
(Signed) *Isabel Jones & Curabel Lee.*

Song Before Supper

Now everything is ready, child, and ready I'm for you,
With supper on the table and a rice-and-radish stew.
And I am even readier to find you ready too,
But all I hear you answer is a
                    Ding-Dang-Dongeroo.

I know you aren't a fireman, and you say you're not a cow.
I think you aren't a cowboy, but I don't know why or how.
And if you're not a lion in the zoo, what *are* you now?
And *is* it Ding-Dang-Dongeroo or
                    Ding-Dang-Dongerow?

You say a thousand other things that I don't understand:
They sound like frogs in water jugs or wind across the sand.
I don't know why you say them, but I wish you'd change
                    your brand.
So Ding-Dang-Dongeroo to you!
            Go wash your other hand!

Perhaps you're just a bicycle, a bittern in the mire,
The hook-and-ladder taking corners flying to a fire,
Lost sheep, or buoys after dark. . . . But won't you *ever*
                    tire
Of Ding-Dang-Dongeroo, young man?
            I do. Sit up, now, *higher!*

I have it! It's a kangaroo! How did I ever miss?
A kangaroo in dungarees! But even so, no bliss
For me to listen all day long to your small orifice
Repeating Ding-Dang-Dongaroo.

Ding-Dang! *Eat some of this!*

Through the Window

The bells are ringing for church this morning,
For church this morning the bells are rung;
And up in the loft the choir is singing,
The choir is singing, the song is sung.

The bells are ringing for church this morning,
A little boy in the seventh pew
Is listening hard to a golden warning:
A bird, perhaps, with a *Where are you?*

Old Tim Toole

The trees are down, but the leaves are up
Says old Tim Toole, the gardener.
Your dog should grow to a nice young pup,
Says old Tim Toole, the gardener.
    But that's the way it is with Tim:
    Everything upside down to him.

Just strike a match: That fire feels good,
Says old Tim Toole, the gardener.
I'll split some ax with the kindling wood,
Says old Tim Toole, the gardener.
    He says things differently, does Tim:
    No topsy-turvy talk for him.

I'll spud the spades, you bean the shells,
Says old Tim Toole, the gardener.
The water hasn't got no wells,
Says old Tim Toole, the gardener.
    All year he talks like that, somehow
    But he's my friend. He's here right now.

A cup of sugar needs some tea,
Says old Tim Toole, the gardener;

With bread inside the meat for me,
Says old Tim Toole, the gardener;
That's how it goes with Tim at lunch.
He lets me share his grapes of bunch.

I'll pump the yellow pickins, son,
Says old Tim Toole, the gardener;
And face a great big cut in one,
Says old Tim Toole, the gardener.
Who hollows pumpkins Halloween?
Old Tim. He says, *The Things I seen!*

You saw a broomstick on a what?
I ask old Tim, the gardener.
He can't tell which is witch. She's got
Some hold on Tim, the gardener.
You see queer things on Halloween?
Tim Toole, I bet, knows what they mean.

V

V
cry the geese
fly V
who me?
rues a goose
no use
for me
to fly a V
I'm only one of three
and three must all agree
if three will make a V
acute or obtuse
with two in the caboose
and one in the
a-po-gee

Song of the Train

Clickety-clack,
Wheels on the track,
This is the way
They begin the attack:
Click-ety-clack,
Click-ety-clack,
Click-ety, *clack*-ety,
Click-ety
Clack.

Clickety-clack,
Over the crack,
Faster and faster
The song of the track:
Clickety-clack,
Clickety-clack,
Clickety, clackety,
Clackety
Clack.

Riding in front,
Riding in back,
Everyone hears
The song of the track:
Clickety-clack,
Clickety-clack,
Clickety, *clickety,*
Clackety
Clack.

Trick or Treat

Halloween,
Halloween,
Halloween!

Latch the latch,
Catch the catch,
Scratch the match.

Witches ride,
Jack will hide
Lantern-eyed.

Better bake.
Better make
Candy, cake.

Mask or sheet:
Trick or treat!
Ghosts are fleet.

Soon or late
Sure as fate
Goes the gate.

Knocker, bell
Cast the spell.
Treat them well!

Silly sooth:
Youth is youth,
Tongue and tooth.

Treat them quick,
Else the trick:
Take your pick!

From the Kitchen: *Ten Poems*

1 Pie

Cross my heart and hope to die
There isn't any in the sky.
There won't be any by and by
Since this one, now, has caught my eye.
There won't be any what? Why, pie —
Pie, pie, pie, *pie*, pie, *pie!*

2 Macaroon

The macaroon is quite "a chewy cookie
Made with sugar, egg whites, almond paste,"
The dictionary says. It should say, "Looky:
I charge one cent to smell it, three to taste."

3 Fudge

Fudge is a kind of chocolate sludge;
It is *not* my favorite candy.
So I am just the one to judge,
If you have a plate of it handy.

4 Peanut Butter

"Peanut butter, considered as a spread. . . ."
"How else could you consider it, my friend?"
"Well, by the spoonful; or, if sick in bed,
By licking it from the index finger's end."

5 Cake

Take cake: a very easy rhyme for bake.
Take icing, which will always rhyme with slicing.
Take filling. Careful now — it rhymes with spilling.
Take crumbs: just as you take them, someone comes.
Take off! That's what you do. For sticky fingers
The rhyme is in the chocolate stain that lingers.

6 Pistachio Ice Cream

Pistachio ice cream, all green;
And I am pausing now between
Two spoonfuls just to say I wish
You had the money for a dish.

7 Animal Crackers

Animal crackers! I ate them years
Before you did. It now appears
That Indian crackers and cowboy cousins
Are eaten by the million dozens.
These new ones may look good to you.
But I am useter to the zoo.

8 *People Crackers*

People crackers! Or don't you know
They make them now for dogs, just so
That poor old Rover can enjoy
A little girl, a little boy,
While you are munching if you please
On lions, tigers, chimpanzees;
On hippos, zebras, tall giraffes;
On mean hyenas full of laughs.

9 *Gingersnaps*

Fresh gingersnaps, bright brittle ones,
Are fine, especially little ones.
Soft gingersnaps uncrunchable
Are totally unmunchable.
Indeed, Pete's father says they are
Inferior to his cigar!
And Peter's father, I've no doubt,
Chewed his cigar to find that out.

10 *Cucumbers vs. Pickles*

Cucumbers always give me squirms:
With them I've *never* come to terms.
But pickles, on the other hand,
The bitter, sweet, the mild, the bland:
Dills, gherkins, fat ones, thin green worms —
Delicious! Do you understand?

Jack, Jill, Spratts, and Horner

"Quick, *quick!*" said Jack.
"Hold back!" said Jill.
That's what they said,
Going up the hill.
Don't think they said
Much after that,

So let's consider
Jack the Spratt,
Who liked the lean,
Which *has* to mean
He left the fat
For Mrs. Spratt.
She fed it, likely,
To the cat —
But we aren't sure of that.
It's *licking* platters
Which *really* matters.

Consider next that brat
I do not care for:
L. J. Horner,
A name cooked up
To rhyme with "corner."
The trouble's with
His thumb, of course.
What slippery plum
Could *one* thumb *force*
To surface from that pie?

"Good boy!" my eye!

Conversation

"Mother, may I stay up tonight?"
"No, dear."
"Oh dear! (She always says 'No, dear').
But Father said I might."
"No, dear."
"He did, that is, if you thought it right."
"No, dear, it isn't right."
"Oh dear! Can I keep on the light?"
"No, dear. In spite
Of what your father said,
You go to bed,
And in the morning you'll be bright
And glad instead
For one more day ahead."
"I might,
But not for one more night."
"No, dear — *no,* dear."
"At least I've been polite, I guess."
"Yes, dear, you've been polite —
Good night."
"Oh dear,
I'd rather stay down here —
I'm quite . . ."
"No, dear. Now, out of sight."
("Well that was pretty near —")
"*Good* night."
("— all right.")
"Good *night!*"

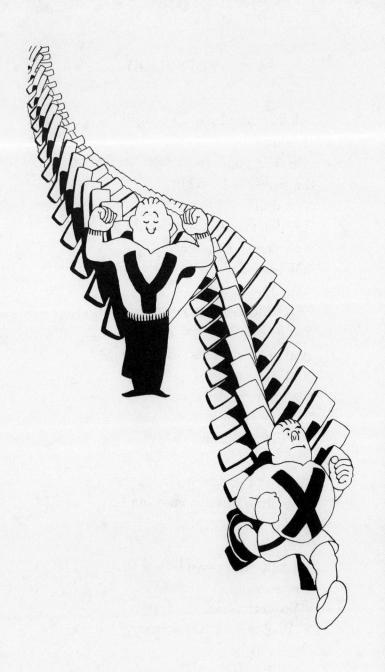

X & Y

Y is a chesty letter,
X is an active one.
Y couldn't stand up better,
X seems to walk or run.
Y is for youth, and youthful
X in his excellent way
Is pleasant. And yet to be truthful,
Child, there will come a day
When, learn as you must, the sequel —
For life has the will to vex —
Nothing for trouble will equal
Your Y and your XY and X.

Z

When all is zed and done,
Z is the letter one.
No other one for me
So lovely as a Z.

Song

Wind and wave and star and sea,
And life is O! a song for me.
Wave and wind and sea and star,
Now I shall tell them what we are.
Star and sea and wind and wave,
I am a giant, strong and brave.
Sea and star and wave and wind,
You are the tiger I have skinned.

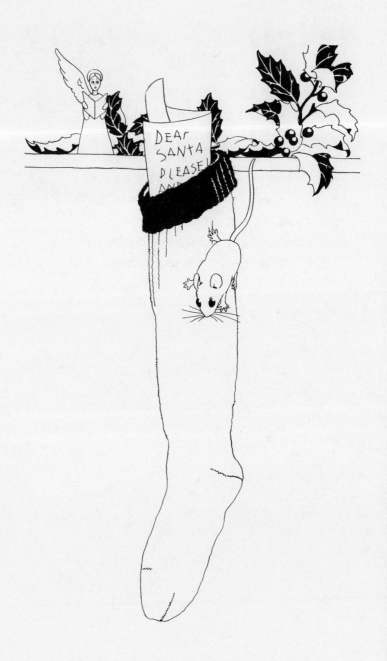

Dear
SANTA
PLEASE

Christmas Eve

I see some waits awaiting,
I hear some singers sing.
Bell-ringers all keep ringing,
But what will Christmas bring?

The air is keen for carols;
My ears are cold, and sting.
Let Peace abide! It's hot inside,
But what will Christmas bring?

I've found a stack of stockings,
An angel with one wing.
By candlelight I've said good night,
But what will Christmas bring?

Noël, Noël! Forever
That bell-like sound a-swing
Is God and love. *I'm* thinking of:
But what will Christmas bring?

Fred

Speaking of Joe, I should have said
Our flying squirrel's name is Fred.

Fred is no flyer, but a glider.
His skin is loose and soft as eider.

But Fred himself is no softy:
He likes tough trees, and likes them lofty.

Fred is not around much at noon;
But at night, and under a bright full moon,

He sails from tree to tree like a circus performer;
And once last summer he sailed right into the dormer

Window of the empty house next door.
But that's Fred all over. Need I say more?

Take Sky

Now think of words. Take *sky*
And ask yourself just why —
Like sun, moon, star, and cloud —
It sounds so well out loud,
And pleases so the sight
When printed black on white.
Take syllable and thimble:
The sound of *them* is nimble.
Take bucket, spring, and dip
Cold water to your lip.
Take balsam, fir, and pine:
Your woodland smell and mine.
Take kindle, blaze, and flicker —
What lights the hearth fire quicker?

Three words we fear but form:
Gale, twister, thunderstorm;
Others that simply shake
Are tremble, temblor, quake.
But granite, stone, and rock:
Too solid, they, to shock.

Put honey, bee, and flower
With sunny, shade, and shower;
Put *wild* with bird and wing,
Put *bird* with song and sing.
Aren't paddle, trail, and camp
The cabin and the lamp?
Now look at words of rest —
Sleep, quiet, calm, and blest;

At words we learn in youth —
Grace, skill, ambition, truth;
At words of lifelong need —
Grit, courage, strength, and deed;
Deep-rooted words that say
Love, hope, dream, yearn, and pray;
Light-hearted words — girl, boy,
Live, laugh, play, share, enjoy.
October, April, June —
Come late and gone too soon.
Remember, words are life:
Child, husband, mother, wife;
Remember, and I'm done:
Words taken one by one

Are poems as they stand —
Shore, beacon, harbor, land;
Brook, river, mountain, vale,
Crow, rabbit, otter, quail;
Faith, freedom, water, snow,
Wind, weather, flood, and floe.
Like light across the lawn
Are morning, sea, and dawn;
Words of the green earth growing —
Seed, soil, and farmer sowing.
Like wind upon the mouth
Sad, summer, rain, and south.
Amen. Put not asunder
Man's *first* word: wonder . . . wonder . . .

Kite

I flew my kite
One bright blue day,
Light yellow-orangey away
Above the tip tall tops of trees,
With little drops from breeze to breeze,
With little rises and surprises,
And the string would sing to these.

I flew my kite
Onc white new day,
Bright orange-yellowy and gay
Against the clouds. I flew it through
The cloudiness of one or two —
Careering, veering, disappearing;
String to fingers, tight and true.

I flew my kite
One dole-dark day,
Dull orange image in the grey,
When not a single bird would fly
So windy wet and wild a sky
Of little languors and great angers.
Kite, *good-by, good-by, good-by!*

Bananas and Cream

Bananas and cream,
Bananas and cream:
All we could say was
Bananas and cream.

We couldn't say fruit,
We wouldn't say cow,
We didn't say sugar —
We don't say it now.

Bananas and cream,
Bananas and cream,
All we could shout was
Bananas and cream.

We didn't say why,
We didn't say how;
We forgot it was fruit,
We forgot the old cow;
We *never* said sugar,
We only said *WOW!*

Bananas and cream,
Bananas and cream;
All that we want is
Bananas and cream!

We didn't say dish,
We didn't say spoon;
We said not tomorrow,
But NOW and HOW SOON

Bananas and cream,
Bananas and cream?
We yelled for bananas,
Bananas and scream!

Scat! Scitten!

Even though
    a cat has a kitten,
    not a rat has a ritten,
    not a bat has a bitten,
    not a gnat has a gnitten,
    not a sprat has a spritten.
    That is that — that is thitten.

Up the Pointed Ladder

Up the pointed ladder, against the apple tree,
One rung, two rungs, what do I see?
A man by the roadside, his eye on me.

Two rungs, three rungs, and so much higher:
I see five miles to the white church spire.
Bet you that man there wishes he were spryer.

Three rungs, four rungs, holding on tight;
Up near the apples now and ready for a bite.
The man by the roadside — is *he* all right?

Four rungs, five rungs — scary, oh my!
There's not much left but the big blue sky,
The faraway mountains, and a wild man's cry.

Five rungs, six rungs. I guess I'm through.
I seem a little dizzy but the apples are too.
And the man yells "Sonny!" and the cow goes "Moo!"

Seven rungs, eight rungs — I can't climb these.
The wobble's in the ladder, it isn't in my knees.
The man cries "Steady, boy!" And up comes a breeze.

Up comes a breezy "Now you come down slow!"
I offer him an apple, but he just won't go.
Well, it's all like that in the world below.

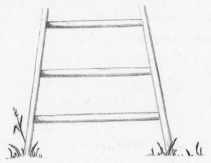

The Importance of Eggs

I've broken lots of eggs, I guess.
The ones in pockets make a mess,
The ones on floors don't clean up well,
The older ones may leave a smell.
Eggs in a bag when dropped won't splash;
The thrown egg will — a yellow smash.
Big double handfuls from the nest
Are eggs that break the easiest.
All boiled eggs shatter. You can peel
The pieces off. I like the feel
Of peeled boiled eggs, but like the look
Of eggs we neither break nor cook —

These incubator eggs in trays
Behind the glass. Whoever stays
Around to see the chicks peck through
Their shells at hatching time? I do.
Of all egg-breakers, Number One
Is Mr. Chick. When he's begun,
And you can see his little bill
Poke, poke, and figure how he will
Turn round inside his prison-house,
As nimble as a nibbling mouse,
Until he's back where he began:
You'll have respect for eggs, young man.
For then, with one good final kick,
There is no egg, but just a chick.

Tooth Trouble

When I see the dentist
I take him all my teeth:
Some of me's above them,
But most of me's beneath.

And one is in my pocket,
Because it grew so loose
That I could fit a string to it
And tighten up the noose.

I'll grow another, dentist says,
And shall not need to noose it.
Another still to drill and fill?
Not me! I won't produce it.

How Tall?

"How tall?" they say.
"You're taller!" they cry.
He stands in the hall
to measure his tall
new tallness.

　　　　All
they do is to lay
a book on his head
so it's good and square
by the door-jamb where
old pencil marks compare.

Such talk, such bustle!
"Don't *lean* on the door,
Don't move a muscle!"
He doesn't.
He thought that he was taller before.
He wasn't.

Wishful

I'd like to slide my sled to bed
And skate myself to school;
I'd like to tame a crow and show
Him off, and make a rule

That rabbits bark and dogs should twitch
Their noses, and that cats
Should fear a mouse. And if the house
Be flittery with bats,

I'd always want it said *How right*
It is that bats can flitter.
Of course this doesn't fit the facts —
But I'm a poor fact-fitter.

Snowman

My little snowman has a mouth,
So he is always smiling south.
My little snowman has a nose;
I couldn't seem to give him toes,
I couldn't seem to make his ears.
He shed a lot of frozen tears
Before I gave him any eyes —
But they are big ones for his size.

I Want You to Meet . . .

. . . Meet Ladybug,
her little sister Sadiebug,
her mother, Mrs. Gradybug,
her aunt, that nice oldmaidybug,
and Baby — she's a fraidybug.

Food and Drink

1 CUP

"Cup, what's up?
Why, it's cocoa scum!
And who likes that?"
"Some."

2 PLATE

"Plate, there's a great
Deal piled on you."
"I know," says Plate,
"But what can *I* do?"

3 KNIFE AND FORK

"Knife, Fork — look,
You're always together."
"So are shepherd and crook,
Stone and brook,
Fish and hook,
Bell and book,
Kitchen, cook,
Umbrella and rainy weather."

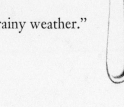

4 NAPKIN

"Napkin, you're slipping.
Why have you no talent for gripping?"
"Why have you no lap,
Quiet, where I can nap?"

5 SAUCER

"Saucer, what's for dessert?"

"Don't ask *me!*
I won't be hurt
To stay clear of dessert.
But let's see:
Could be prunes, I guess.
Yes, could be prunes."

"Noon's not the time to have . . . what?"

"I forgot —
I always forget, meal to meal.
Saucers can't *feel,*
We just fill
Or we spill.
Here it comes."

"Golly, *plums!*"

6 TABLE

"Table, I've got my eye on you,
Hoping there may be pie on you.
And if there isn't, fie on you!
Right now there's a fly on you."

7 PITCHER

"Pitcher,
You unreliable switcher
from milk to water to lemonade
which I shall grade:

1) lemonade

2) milk

3) water,

Glass, your daughter,
is asking for you.
Shall I pour you?"

8 JAM

"Spread," said Toast to Butter,
And Butter spread.
"That's better, Butter,"
Toast said.

"Jam," said Butter to Toast.
"Where are you, Jam,
When we need you most?"
Jam: "Here I am,

Strawberry, trickly and sweet.
How are you, Spoon?"
"I'm helping somebody eat,
I think, pretty soon."

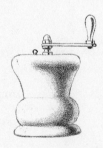

9   SALT AND PEPPER

"Why," says Salt to Pepper,
"are we always separate —
I in my cellar;
and you, poor feller,
in a box, mill, or grinder?
It would be kinder
to let you loose."

"No use," says Pepper:
"You take life easy,
I make life sneezy.
Why, damp or dry,
there you lie;
but if I let fly,
people cry."

"I see," says Salt.
"Not your fault,
I suppose.
You're O.K. by me;
so is sugar in tea.
And so it goes.
But then,
I've no nose."

10   JUG AND MUG

"Jug, aren't you fond of Mug?"
"Him I could hug," said Jug.
"Mug, aren't you fond of Jug?"
"Him I could almost slug!"
"Humph," said Jug with a shrug.
"When he pours, he goes *Glug!*" said Mug.
" Well, *I* don't spill on the rug," said Jug.
"Smug old Jug," said Mug.
"I'll fill you, Mug," said Jug.
"*Will*, will you, Jug!" said Mug.
"Don't be ugly," said Jug juggly
"Big lug," said Mug.
Glug.

So Run Along and Play

You might think I was in the way.
So run along — along with what?
There isn't much that I have got
To run along with or beside.
The door, of course, is open wide;
The day, of course, is clear and fine;
The time right now, I guess, is mine.

But what is there to run to?
It wouldn't be much fun to
Run along — well, just to run.
O.K. for two or three; I'm *one*,
I'm all alone. I guess I'll walk
Along. I'll stop somewhere and talk;
Perhaps I'll think where I can walk to,
Because that's where there's what I'll talk to.
I'll walk along, but I won't play;
I won't play I am playing. Way
Beyond the third house one block back's
Another house with funny cracks
Across the paint. It seems to me
That's where some painter ought to be.

He should have been there years ago;
Maybe they don't like painters, though.
Or maybe he has my complaint:
They said "So run along and paint."
Well, if he ran along like me,
I'll bet I may know where he'll be.

Squaw Talk

I see a lot of cowboys.
Have they ever seen a cow?
I hear a lot of gunfire
In a shabby sort of row,
All answering some podners primed
With something that goes *Pow!*

I see a lot of Indians —
No wigwam or canoe.
And sleepy in my teepee
I am not much likely to,
For squaws who play with Indians
Are very, very few.

Come Christmas snow, while wranglers wear
New chaps and stuff astride
The TV range, in turtleneck
And ski pants far outside,
With twinkly spurs and a bouncy grey,
Through the wide white fields I ride.

Man for Mars

Spaced in a helmet
now his head
still has a mouth
which must be fed,

still has two eyes
for looking round,
still has big ears
but little sound;

still has a nose
that runs a bit —
no spaceman blows
or scratches it;

still has two hands
which he employs
in picking apples;
still enjoys

the heady smell
of autumn air —

especially heady
inside there.

Apples! Some wormy,
mostly beauties.
His inter-
planetary duties

over now, let
Mars and Cygnus-
X relax;
too much of bigness,

too much of all
this interstellar
business tires
a busy feller.

Here is a barn
and here is sun:
a combination
darn good fun;

a spaceman's helmet
full of Macs,

free oxygen
the cosmos lacks;

white teeth, an apple,
the heaven's dome,
and a hornet blasting
off for home.

Sailor John

Young Stephen has a young friend John
Who in his years is getting on.
He's getting on for six, I think,
Or seven. Yes, he's on the brink
Of seven, which is pretty old
Unless you're eight or nine all told.
But anyhow, John has a notion
That he would like to sail the ocean.
He has the notion, understand,
But *not* the ocean — just the land.
John hasn't any boat as yet,
Although his feet are often wet:
They're wet today because of rain.
Quite right — he can't go out again
Unless he finds some other shoes.
John has a notion he will choose
To stay inside and shut the door
And lie right down upon the floor
And think about the ocean, how
It's not available just now;
And think about the kinds of boat
He doesn't have that wouldn't float.

153

Sing-Song

Clocks
are full of tocks.
When they stop
the trick's
to fix the ticks.
Tick-tock
G'long!
says the clock.

Clip-clop —
that's the horse,
of course.
A flick of the whip
and he goes at a good fast clip.
If his clop goes too,
he hasn't lost a shoe.

Ding!
hear the bell ring?
clapper in the mouth
swinging north and south,
swinging up and down,
ding-dong over the town.
If something's wrong,
it's *always* in the dong.

Where?

Where is that little pond I wish for?
Where are those little fish to fish for?

Where is my little rod for catching?
Where are the bites that I'll be scratching?

Where is my rusty reel for reeling?
Where is my trusty creel for creeling?

Where is the line for which I'm looking?
Where are those handy hooks for hooking?

Where is the worm I'll have to dig for?
Where are the boots that I'm too big for?

Where is there *any* boat for rowing?
Where is . . . ?
                    Well, anyway, it's snowing.

You Mustn't Call It Hopsichord

You mustn't call it *hopsichord*,
It's not played by a toad.

You mustn't say a *chevaleer* —
It wasn't he who rode.

It's *sacred* to the memory of,
Not *scared*, as you prefer.

You put apostrophes in *we're*
And keep them out of *were*.

Un*durfed?* No, no, it's under*fed;*
Bed-raggled isn't right, I said.

You *shirr* an egg — how could you shear it?
Music's not hominy or grits;

The thing is *ferret*, though you fear it;
Twist *twist*, and twist is *twits*.

Please never say again you're *mizzled;*
Mis-led you are, or led astray.

The word is wizened and not *wizzled;*
Hens don't lie down — they *lay*.

Spelling Bee

It takes a good speller
to spell *cellar*,
separate, and *benefiting*;
not omitting
cemetery, *cataclysm*,
picknicker and *pessimism*.
And have you ever tried
innocuous, *inoculate*,
dessert, *deserted*, *desiccate*;
divide and *spied*,
gnat, *knickers*, *gnome*,
crumb, *crypt*, and *chrome*;
surreptitious, *supersede*,
delete, *dilate*, *impede*?

Castor Oil

Ever, ever, not ever so terrible
Stuff as unbearable castor oil
Deep in the glass
Like a chew of cheese,
Like a squeal of brass-bound
Antifreeze.
And round the rim
Of the glass a squeeze
Of orange and lemon.
But will they please
Not say "Delicious!"
And "You won't taste it!"
It's just as vicious
As when *they* faced it.

Three Signs of Spring

Kite on the end of the twine,
Fish on the end of a line,
Dog on the end of a whine.

Dog on the leash is straining,
Fish on the line is gaining:
Only these two complaining.

Kite is all up in the air,
Kite doesn't quite compare,
Kite doesn't *really* care.

Kite, of course, is controllable;
Dog, with a word, consolable;
Fish hopes he isn't poleable.

Trust the dog for an urge,
Trust the kite for a surge,
Trust the trout to submerge.

Kite in the wind and the rain,
Dog in the woods again,
Fish in his deep domain.

Starling

In burnished armor
with yellow lance
a knighted starling
now perchance

stiff-legged unhorsed
but bold as brass
steps from his stirrups
across the grass.

No guile has he
nor sword nor shield;
he levels with
his lance the field.

Pigeon and sparrow
yield him way
unmailed unequal
each are they;

whatever it is
they pick to peck
Sir Starling will
in person check.

Cold iridescence
in the sun
he sweeps the terrace
with his Begone!

For certes court
and kingdom lie
wherever birds
will flock and fly.

Afreet

Afreet I am afraid of:
I don't know what he's made of.
I don't know where he hides,
Or maybe just abides,
Or maybe has a haunt.
Whatever does he want?
I don't know what he does,
Or if he is or was.
I don't know how he looks;
He's giving me the shooks.
I think he's a jinnee —
You know what *that* would be!
A giant among jinn,
A groan to end a grin,
A shriek to still a sigh,
A croak to kill a cry.
Afreet gives me a fright:
I'm glad he's out of sight.

Alley Cat

His nightly song will scarce be missed:
Nine times death claimed our alley cat.
Good-by, you old somnambulist! —
A long word, that.

Mr. Halloween

He has no broomstick, but you dare not say
Jack Pumpkinhead and he are not old friends.
He has the last word there with Jack — the way
He flickers with Jack's light in candle-ends.

One sheet makes quite a ghost of Tom or Jill;
But Tom and Jill are real and go about
Their night's work putting scare into the shrill
Still younger Toms and Jills who may be out —

Not seeing Mr. Halloween, who bides
His time in some tree's knothole, in some crack
Where *was* a door once: So he often hides
To send the shivers up and down Tom's back.

Or croaks to Jill from nowhere. "Who was that?"
She cries. No . . . nothing . . . nothing . . . all in fun.
But *was* it? Through the shadow flits a bat.
And those two witches! Now there's only *one*.

Sly Mr. Halloween! Don't trust him, Joan.
He's in the dark glass, searching through your mask.

He was that rustle in the leaves, your own
(You *thought* your own) dry voice. Don't ever ask

Strange characters in cloak and hat if they
Are so-and-so, for one may vanish quick
Before your eyes. Be careful how you say
All words that sound like *Boo!* Don't ever lick

The candied apple which he may have seen.
Be wary of those bubbles in a jug
Of cider — just like Mr. Halloween
To be the one you pour into your mug.

Good luck this chancy night! Be sure to wear
Your ring on backwards, or to point your toes
In, *in* — not out — when something skitters. *Scare!*
That's Mr. Halloween. But *when?* Who knows!

Write Me a Verse

I've asked Professor Swigly Brown
To talk about four kinds of Rime,
If you will kindly settle down.
You won't? Well, then, some other time. . . .

PROFESSOR BROWN: The simplest of all verse to write is the
couplet. There is no argument about
this: it *is* the simplest. I have said so.

Couplet

1

A couplet is two lines — two lines in rime.
The first comes easy, the second may take time.

2

Most couplets will have lines of equal length;
This gives them double dignity and strength.

3

Please count the syllables in 2 and say
How many. Ten each line? Correct! And they

4

In turn comprise the five-foot standard line:
Pentameter. The foot's *iambic.* Fine

5

Enough! On human feet, of course, our shoes
Do match; likewise the laces. If you choose

6

A briefer line,
Like this of mine,

7

Or say
O.K.

8

Why, *these* are couplets, somewhat crude but true
To form. Try one yourself. See how you do.

9

Meanwhile, I'll give *you* one. Hand me that pen.
A four-foot line — eight syllables, not ten:

10

I cán / not síng / the óld / songs nów;
I név / er could / sing án / y hów.

11

Couplets, you see, should make their stand alone.
I've used some differently, but that's my own

12

responsibility.

PROFESSOR BROWN: We come now to the second easiest form of verse: the quatrain. Since the quatrain in length equals *two* couplets, it ought to be just twice as easy to write. It isn't . . . it isn't.

Quatrain

1

When there is more to say — or more than planned —
A couplet's very easy to expand.
Expansive couplets, then, if out of hand,
May nicely run to four lines. Understand?

2

Four lines — quatrain; long lines or short,
But *good* lines, with a good report
Of one another as they progress.
Note one / an oth / er for change / of stress

3

Or emphasis: the sudden sharpening pace.
A quatrain says its say with perfect grace.
"I strove with none, for none was worth my strife" —
First line of four* to haunt you all your life.

---

* Inquire of Walter Savage Landor in *Bartlett's Familiar Quotations*.

I'll not attempt a long example —
I mean with lines of many feet;
But still you ought to have a sample
Or two to prove the form *is* neat.

5

Here goes:
Suppose
Suppose
Suppose

6

The ship sails for Spain,
For Spain the ship sails;
You can't go by train,
For a train runs on rails.

Let's sail a ship for far-off Spain;
We really can't get there by train.
But still a big ship has no sails;
Why not a train that has no rails?

Note rimes in 1 — the rime control is *planned*.
In 2, *two* pairs of rimes; in 6 we find
abab (*Spain, sails, train, rails*). Last kind
Is this (abba): *planned, find, kind, and*

Forget that ship that has no sails.
Let's jet by plane across to Spain
Above the sea they call the Main.
(Say something here that rimes with *sails*.)

PROFESSOR BROWN: The limerick, by all odds, is the most popular short verse form in English. Hundreds of people write hundreds of wretched limericks every day. Somehow they fail to understand that the limerick, to be lively and successful, *must* have *perfect* riming and *flawless* rhythm. The limerick form is far older than Edward Lear (1812-1888), but it was he who first made it popular.

1

A limerick shapes to the eye
Like a small very squat butterfly,
    With its wings opened wide,
    Lots of nectar inside,
And a terrible urge to fly high.

2

The limerick's lively to write:
Five lines to it — all nice and tight.
    Two long ones, two trick
    Little short ones; then quick
As a flash here's the last one in sight.

3

Some limericks — most of them, reely —
Make rimes fit some key word like *Greely*
    (A man) of *Dubuque*
    (Rimed with cucumber — cuque)
Or a Sealyham (dog). Here it's *Seely*.

4

There once was a scarecrow named Joel
Who couldn't scare crows, save his soel.
    But the crows put the scare
    Into Joel. He's not there
Any more. That's his hat on the poel.

5

"There was an old man" of wherever
You like, thus the limerick never
    Accounts for the young:
    You will find him unsung
Whether stupid, wise, foolish, or clever.

6

There was a young man, let me say,
Of West Pumpkinville, Maine, U.S.A.
        You tell me there's not
        Such a place? Thanks a lot.
I forget what he did anyway.

7

Take the curious case of Tom Pettigrew
And Hetty, his sister. When Hettigrew
        As tall as a tree
        She came just to Tom's knee.
And did *Tom* keep on growing? You bettigrew.

8

Consider this odd little snail
Who lives on the rim of a pail:
        Often wet, never drowned,
        He is always around
Safe and sound, sticking tight to his trail.

9

A man who was fond of his skunk
Thought he smelled pure and pungent as punk.
    But his friends cried No, no,
      No, no, no, no, no, *no!*
He just stinks, or he stank, or he stunk.

10

There was an old man who cried Boo!
Not to me or to he but to you.
    He also said scat
      To a dog not a cat,
And to Timbuc he added too-too.

11

It's been a bad year for the moles
Who live just in stockings with holes;
    And bad for the mice
      Who prefer their boiled rice
Served in shoes that don't have any soles.

There once was a man in the Moon,
But he got there a little too soon.

    Some others came later

    And fell down a crater —

When *was* it? Next August? Last June?

"This season our tunnips was red
And them beets was all white. And instead

    Of green cabbages, what

    You suspect that we got?"

"I don't know." "Didn't plant none," he said.

I don't much exactly quite care
For these cats with short ears and long hair;

    But if anything's worse

    It's the very reverse:

Just you ask any mouse anywhere.

So by chance it may be you've not heard
Of a small sort of queer silent bird.
    Not a song, trill, or note
    Ever comes from his throat.
If it does, I take back every word.

16

Write a limerick now. Say there was
An old man of some place, what he does,
    Or perhaps what he doesn't,
    Or isn't or wasn't.
Want help with it? Give me a buzz.

PROFESSOR BROWN: The triolet is another brief verse form, no longer popular and not too easy to write, even though it *looks* easy. The rime-scheme (end words) is abaaabab. That is, in example 1 the rimes will repeat in that order:

droll	(a)	soul	(a)
repeat	(b)	feet	(b)
control	(a)	droll	(a)
droll	(a)	repeat	(b)

Please observe that the first (a) rime-word (droll) and the first (b) rime-word (repeat) occur again: *droll* in lines 4 and 7; *repeat* in line 8. Mr. Mc-Cord has taken a few small liberties with some of his triolets which follow — but he shouldn't have. I think he knows better; but for the moment, shame on him! Stick to the rules.

1

The triolet's droll;
You must watch it repeat
The lines in control.
The triolet's droll
With a brightness of soul,
With such swift little feet!
The triolet's droll;
You must watch it repeat.

2

The birds in the feeder
are fighting again.
Not squirrels in the cedar,

but birds in the feeder.
They haven't a leader:
just eight, nine, or ten
of the birds in the feeder
are fighting again.

3

The swallows all twitter
In line on the wire.
Each fatter and fitter,
The swallows all twitter:
Old sitter, young sitter,
Madáme and Esquíre.
The swallows all twitter
In line on the wire.

4

Eggs are all runny,
Though legs they have none.
It's terribly funny
That eggs are all runny!
When laid by a bunny
For Easter, not one

Of *his* eggs are all runny:
They roll and *we* run.

5

It's a foggy day
When winter thaws
And the snow is grey.
It's a foggy day:
O Doggy, go 'way
With your dirty paws!
It's a foggy day
When winter thaws.

6

I fed some cheese
To the cellar mice.
It went like a breeze
When I fed some cheese;
And they came by threes
And they came in a trice
When I fed some cheese
To the cellar mice.

Thank you, thank you, Professor Brown!
You've made us feel all upside down,
All inside out, all backside to —
But that's what you are paid to do.

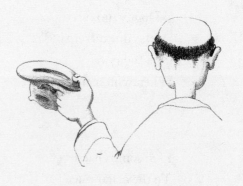

A Fool and His Money

Looking back over the years,
Nothing now seems so sad,
So much a matter of tears,
As the little gold piece I had:
Gold piece and a five-dollar bill,
And tell you of them I will.

The little gold piece was small,
Worth five times fifty cents;
You may say it was nothing at all,
But to me oh, immense, immense.
And it was; for what else indeed
Could I ever want or need?

One little gold piece the size
Of a penny — there aren't any now —
And deep in the pocket to prize.
So I remember how

And where and exactly when,
When I was twelve or ten,

In the observation car
Of our California train
I sat out back; and far
Behind me slid the plain.
And what would become of me
In the land where I was to be?

I tossed a penny to see:
Heads for a happy life.
"What would become of me?"
Went through me like a knife.
A penny flew into space.
What penny! No trace, no trace.

It was like the five-dollar bill
Before we took to the West.
Aunt Mary: I see her still
At the station, departing guest,
With a crisp new five and a kiss.
But in my delirious bliss

I ran up and down till (the train
Coming in) I was caught by the hand,
And the bill made a green little stain
In the steam and the wind. I must stand
And wait till the train took Aunt Mary.
Five dollars? No trace — nary, nary.

I Have a Book

that has no cover
where there used to be a lady
and her knighted lover.
Oh, her lover was a knight
and his armor fitted right.
While he hadn't any horse,
still I always thought he might;
and I always thought of course
he'd be riding far away,
for the day was good and bright
though the tree was big and shady.
Now there isn't any lady
and there isn't any knight,
and there never was a horse,
so there never was a fight.
And the book all by itself
is sort of lonely on the shelf.

Little League

Those eager Little Leaguers,
Terry Quince and Donald Spratt!
Take Terry out in left field, and
Take Donald up at bat:
Cubs vs. Dalton's Cringers.
Don's a Cub — but you know that.

His bat is fast, far-reaching;
He has knocked a long fly out
To left field, which is Terry's
Territory round about.
Up now goes Terry's hand to shield
His blue eyes from the sun,

Which looks much like the baseball,
Only redder. He takes one,
Two, three, four, five, six, seven strides —
He doesn't need all these.
It seems the silly baseball rides
An unassisted breeze.

The moment's tense, he's near the fence!
His mitt could squeeze the ball with ease,
If he could spear it curving near.
But what prevents (no fan can sense)

Is Terry-trouble in the knees;
Loud buzzing in his ears, like bees,

The ball drops dead. Does Terry
Chase it swiftly, as he ought,
With Donald racing round from
First to second? Ball's not caught,
Not even noticed. Terry lies
Face downward on the green,

And pounds his fists and sobs
For shame, while Donald streaks between
Third base and home. I'm sorry
To report that dismal scene.
I rather wish I'd told what *Terry*
Did at bat, I mean.

The final score was Don's Cubs four,
With Dalton's Cringers somewhat more,
Since Terry homered with one on.
He topped the Stoppy Shoppy screen,
Which pleased him so he grinned at Don.

The two teams' errors, seventeen.

Sally Lun Lundy

Barefoot Monday
For Sally Lun Lundy;
Stocking-day, shoes-day
All day Tuesday.
A rather loose-ends day
Turns up Wednesday.
Not-a-leaf-stirs-day
Well through Thursday.
Lowest low-tide-day
Wading on Friday.
Solemn old Saturday:
Raindrops-splatter-day.

What about Sunday,
Sally Lun Lundy?

Mingram Mo

There was a man named Mingram Mo
Who never knew just where to go.
Mo had a friend — I forget his name —
Who never knew from whence he came.
And then Mo's sister, Mrs. Kriss,
Would misremember most of this,
And say to Mingram: "Mingram Mo,
What is it that you never know?
And who's this friend who knows it less?"
(His name still slips me, I confess.)
Whereat poor Mingram would invent
A place to go to when he went,
Wherein his friend called — never mind —
Might feel quite not so left behind.
But where *that* was, his sister Mrs.
Kriss still misremembers. This is
All that you will ever know of
Mingram Mo, by Jove, by Jo-of.

Down by the Sea

Everybody's in the ocean,
Everybody's gone to sail;
Everybody's rubbing lotion.
Where is Johnny? Here's his pail.

Every kind of beach umbrella,
Every sort of bouncy ball;
Johnny wades an archipela-
go of rocky islands, all

Razored barnacles as thickly
Spread as freckles on your face.
Johnny doesn't care partickly,
Splashing Sammy's sister Grace;

Or it may be Sammy's brother —
Down by the sea they're much the same.
Someone's aunt is someone's mother,
No one's dad is glad he came.

Every boy has dug a tunnel,
Built a castle, buried Pop;
Every girl thinks Oh, what fun'll
I have barefoot — slop, slop, slop!

Everybody's wet and sandy,
Everybody's fat or thin;
Johnny lets his soggy candy
Drip and dribble down the chin.

Every picnic spot is where a
Youngster running by can spread
Something of the soft Sahara
Over something that was bread.

Everybody's got a tiny
Radio that blares the news;
Everybody beached or briny
Sweats or shivers, smokes or chews.

Everybody's Coke is fizzy,
Everybody's towel is damp.
See where Johnny's . . . O.K., is he?
I *can't* turn: I've got a cramp.

Everybody's hallelujah
Isn't everybody's dish.
Everybody, then: here's to ya,
Johnny's found a stinking fish.

Books

Like their looks?
Readers read them in nooks,
in a hammock, in bed, up the stair,
in a chair, on the porch; anywhere
on the floor, by the shore,
in a plane, on a train;
by the pool, a big rock,
in a room with no clock;
in a bus, trailer, tent;
in a Laundromat meant
for a book; under trees;
on long trips overseas;
in their bath in a tub —
I suppose turning on with their toes
the hot water. Who knows?
Books don't tell you to scrub.

You exist? Want to *be*?
Not with comics, cheap movies, commercial TV.
No, you won't! Only books — the *real* books —
set their hooks in your brain:
without them, you'll slide down the drain;
and at twenty,

as plenty today do,
have Mickey-Mouse minds,
as (I hate to say) *they* do.

One tells by the looks
of most people if books
are a part of their life.
Papers, magazines, rife
in this world, help to kill
time *and* books. But until
you can judge for yourself
of the best on the shelf,
books won't feed you. They *can*:
boy and girl; woman, man.

Just begin when you're young:
when a book in your eye
seems as tall as the sky;
when words, *words* in their flight
are as birds in your sight;
when it thrills you to find
you are using your mind,
and inside it is what
someone else hasn't got.

You! Begin when you're young,
when the tip of your tongue

is still limber. Books reach
with the splendor of speech.
Who can say things well said
is well read.

Real among the realest books: *Treasure Island, Far Away
and Long Ago, Alice, The Wizard of Oz, The Wind in
the Willows, Life on the Mississippi, The Oregon Trail,
Cache Lake Country, The Mirror of the Sea, The Mys-
terious Island, Robinson Crusoe, Red Fox, Arctic Wild,
The Matchlock Gun, The Rescuers, Jeremy, Those Were
the Sioux, Tarka the Otter, The Thirteen Clocks, Char-
lotte's Web, Piping Down the Valleys Wild, The Golden
Book of Verse, Fun and Nonsense, Come Hither, The
Crock of Gold, Imagination's Other Place, The Riddle
of the Sands, The Railway Children, The Dog Who
Wouldn't Be, A Care for Nature, The Small Years, The
Lost World, Huckleberry Finn, The Sea and The Jungle,
Kim, Sherlock Holmes, Delight, The Outermost House,
Under the Tree,* Edward Lear's *Nonsense Books, The
Country of the Pointed Furs, A Professor of Life.*

Spike Spoke Spook

There was this Spike who simply could not fit
First letters to his words. The word *commit*,
For instance, came out *ommit*. It was kook
To see his writing. Take these lines: pure spook!

here as his pike ho imply ould ot it
irst etters o is ords. he ord *ommit*,
or nstance, ame ut *ommit.* t as ook
o ee is riting. ake hese ines: ure pook!

So when your mother says, "It's supper time,"
Be glad that you're not sitting down to rhyme:
o hen our other ays "t's upper ime,"
e lad hat ou're ot itting own o hyme!

Queer

I seem to see
in the apple tree,
I seem to know
from the field below,
I seem to hear
when the woods are near,
I seem to sense
by the farmer's fence,
I seem to place
just the faintest trace,
I seem to smell
what I can't quite tell,
I seem to feel
that it isn't real,
I seem to guess
at it, more or less.

Alphabet
(Eta Z)

1

A is one
And we've begun.

2

B is two —
Myself and you.

3

C is three —
You, who? and me.

4

D is four;
Let's close the door.

5

E is five
Bees in a hive.

6

F is six
Fat candlesticks.

7

G is seven
And not eleven.

8

H is eight,
And gaining weight.

9

I is nine,
Of slender spine;

10

J is ten.
And then what? Then

11

Comes K eleven
Which isn't seven.

12

L is twelve,
Or two-thirds elve.

13

M thirteen
Stands in between

14

Your A, my Z.
N's fourteen. We

15

Now come to O;
Fifteen or so —

16

Fifteen, I guess;
P Sixteen. Yes,

17

Since seventeen
Cries Q for Queen!

18

Eighteen is R,
The end of star;

19

Nineteen is S
As in success;

20

T's twenty, twice
What ten was; nice

21

To add one to
And capture U,

22

Or add a pair
That V can share.

23

Your twenty-three's
In wow! Xerxes

24

Shows X the core
Of twenty-four.

25

Y keeps alive
In twenty-five;

26

Z's in a fix:
Poor twenty-six!

Snake

Very thin
and opaque
is the skin
of a snake.

Let it shed,
Let it wane
to this dead
cellophane.

Let it be:
I've no itch
to see
which is which.

Up from Down Under

The boomerang and kangaroo
comprise a very pleasant two;
The coolibah and billabong
together make a sort of song.
But tasty as a fresh meringue
is billabong with boomerang;
and better than hooray-hoorah
is kangaroo with coolibah.

The Cove

The cove is where the swallows skim
And where the trout-rings show,
And where the bullfrog hugs the rim
Of lily pads; and so
The million wake, as hatching flies
Hatch out into a world of eyes,
A world of wing and mouth and fin,
Of feathers, scales, and froggy skin.

A tough old world that *they* are in!

Glowworm

Never talk down to a glowworm —
Such as *What do you knowworm?*
How's it down belowworm?
Guess you're quite a slowworm.
No. Just say
         Helloworm!

Hitchhiker

There was a witch who met an owl.
He flew beside her, wing to jowl.

Owl language always pleased the witch:
Her owl at home sat in his niche
And talked a lot about the bats
He met at night, and how the cats
Were scared of him. That sort of thing.
But here was one owl on the wing,
Who said — I don't mean said "Who, who!" —
Who said, "I've just escaped the zoo.
I'm going home. I haven't flown
Much lately — that is, on my own.
They flew me to the zoo, you know,
Last . . . well, it's several years ago.

"My wings are stiff: I'm tired! *Am* I!
So when I saw you flying by,
I thought 'She's heading north by east.
If I can hitch a ride at least
As far as Pocono, I'll make
It home.' Okay? Is that a rake
Or broom you're flying? Sure! A broom.

I see it is. Nice model. Room
Enough along the handle for
An owl to perch. Thanks! You can pour
It on! A little shut-eye's what
I need."
       I guess that's what he got.

Witch's Broom Notes

1

On Halloween, what bothers some
About these witches is, how come
In sailing through the air like bats
They never seem to lose their hats?

2

Hitchhiking owls, as we have seen,
Ride nicely on this queer machine.
Black cats have been reported too;
Which isn't possible or true.

3

Another thing: if brooms can fly,
Do witches keep them handy-by
To sweep the kitchen floor with, say?
Or do they have them locked away
For private passage through the sky?

4

All witches ride well forward, aim
Their broomstick handles, make no claim
For anything like magic jet.
Who knows a witch's airspeed yet?

Pumpkin Seeds

1

There is a man who says he may
Have on the market any day
A pumpkin of tremendous size,
With precut mouth and nose and eyes.
He says his pumpkin grows that way,
Unlike the ones for pumpkin pies.
And I suppose he'll win a prize —
But not if some kids have their say!

2

Just dwelling on that thought above:
Why, half the total pleasure of
The days approaching Halloween
Is when we cut the nose between
The mouth and eyes in yellow head,
Or put the nose in first instead;
Then make the mouth and eyes. I mean,
We bring alive a thing that's dead,
And do it with a sense of love.

3

A ghost can be a scary thing:
A pillowcase won't do.
A ghost should be an airy thing
A man can look right through.
There's lots too much of some for that.
Ghosts need to starve. Is yours too fat?
Will lookers look and laugh at you?

Mom's Mums

Here she comes!
Who? Mom's who! Mom's best mums,
along with glads, cukes, spuds, and plums,
are what she's got today for sale
beside the road. Mom's mums are pale
plain yellow, white, deep orange. Psalms
could not describe these mums of Mom's,
a lady favored with green thumbs
for glads, cukes, spuds, grass, plums. But mum's
the word with Mom. Somehow it sums
This little burst of flower bombs.

Who down in Florida with palms
can't hear the Yankee sound of drums?

"Come by, come by, come buy Mom's mums!"

Goose, Moose & Spruce

Three gooses: geese.
Three mooses: meese?
Three spruces: spreece?

Little goose: gosling.
Little moose: mosling?
Little spruce: sprosling?

Dr. Klimwell's Fall

(A poem to be read aloud)

> We wake and find our-
> selves on a stair; there
> are stairs below us . . .
> there are stairs above us,
> many a one, which go
> upward and out of sight.
> — RALPH WALDO EMERSON

Down the star-stairs fell
Old Dr. I. Klimwell.
What he was doing there,
Climbing that kind of stair,
Staring down starry stone,
Standing (trust him) alone,
No one will ever know.
Stars, when you have to go
Where Dr. Klimwell did,
Hide away — hidden, hid
Under some stellar door;
But, if you've been before
(Doctors, of course, *have* been)
Knock, and they'll let you in.

Going up, going down
Clean through the heart of town,
Up through the cloudy rug,
Down through the cave undug,
Right where you want to stop;
Star-stairs to bottom, top —
Either way, there they are,
Stairs of the stepping-star.

Old Dr. Klimwell, he —
Much, very much like me;
Much, very much as you —
Liked the same things you do:
People afloat on rafts,
Dust in the sunlit shafts
Shining through colored panes,
Little dogs not on chains,
Little boys out for trout,
Little girls flumped about,
Stores where they sell you stuff,
Seas when they aren't too rough,
Kites when they scrape the sky,
Trees when the leaves let fly;
Trains coming round the curve,
Indians in reserve,

Dolls with their shoes laced right,
Whistles blown late at night —
Whistles one *ought* to hear
When Dr. Klimwell's near —
Lanterns and shouting men,
Roosters but not the hen,
Ducks on the pond; long lakes,
Snowfall in fat wet flakes,
Circuses, clowns, and stunts,
Hands that you held to once,
Holes in the dead tree trunk,
Stones down the well *kerplunk*,
Moss round a mountain bog,
Leopard frogs, bull frogs, frog;
Sodas with triple straws,
Crows with black throaty *caws*,
Rabbits — with twitchy nose,
Places where no one goes;
Birches to climb and swing,
Geese in the sky for spring,
Feel of wet sand on feet,
Dusk down a city street;
Things worlds and winds away
Turning up night and day,

Turning up soon or late,
Turning up while you wait.

Well, that is quite a list
(Not very much I've missed)
Made so you'll understand
What Dr. Klimwell *and*
You and I think about
All day in, all day out.
Little things, some would say.
Happy things, though, *aren't* they?

"There now, at last!" would cry
Old Dr. Klimwell. "My,
My, my, my, *my!* I smell
Leaves burning. Must be well
On towards . . . eh? . . . Halloween?
What is there in between?"
"Nothing. For someone's sick.
Climb, Dr. Klimwell, *quick!*"
Who could be sick above
Whom we'd be thinking of
Not knowing why or where
One could be sick up there?
Quick as the flight of thieves

Right by the rake of leaves,
Spiraling through the clear
Leaf-empty trees appear
Stones for the Doctor's climb
Time after sudden time,
Just when your laggard glance
Spies, as it will by chance,
Something you want to see:
Dragonflies floating knee-
High over sandy shore;
Something behind the door,
Something inside of tents,
Something that won't make sense,
Something before your face,
Something from outer space,
Something you've heard of, just —
Something the rain might rust,
Something you don't quite trust,
Something . . .

Many Crows, Any Owl

Caw, caw, *caw!* . . .
Come see them fly.
There's an owl up there
In the tree nearby:

In the big lone oak
With its leaves all brown,
Where the caw-caw-*caws*
Call the old owl down.

But the old owl sits
Till he drops one lid
Over one wide eye:
"Which is *what* I did?"

"Which is you're an owl
Same as we are crows."
So the cause of the caw-caw-
Caws, he goes

To another tree
Near another farm.

There's another great big black
Fresh alarm.

"Oh, but no you don't,"
Says the owl this time.
"There's a man with a gun,
And a crow is prime

"Good reason why
He is out just now,
When he might be thinking
About the cow,

"Or about the calf,
Or the five big geese,
Or the pumpkins just
Up the road a piece.

"But he's after *you*
And your caw-caw noise.
So I'm going to sleep.
Good morning, boys!"

Crickets

all busy punching tickets,
clicking their little punches.
The tickets come in bunches,
good for a brief excursion,
good for a cricket's version
of travel (before it snows) to
the places a cricket goes to.
Alas! the crickets sing alas
in the dry September grass.
Alas, alas, in every acre,
every one a ticket-taker.

The Leaves

When the leaves are young,
Shaped to the tip of tongue,
They do not speak at all.

All summer, green and spread
Sun-dappled overhead,
They talk . . . talk on and on . . .

On days of gentle weather
They whisper, tongues together,
Breathe, meditate, and stir.

Were ever clouds so sure
That clouds will long endure?
Not ever, leaves say. No.

No matter what? In rain
The dripping-leaf refrain
Repeats the pretty patter:

No matter, matter . . . Storm
Takes leaves like bees in swarm —
The sullen swirl in flight.

Light tongues, so bidden bold,
Sting, quiver, lash, and scold.
No matter matter what,

Not death for us, they cry!
But by and by and by
Comes autumn loping lean

Between the woods and village.
Red, yellow, gold, her pillage . .
The sickled fingers . . . Down

Down flutters every leaf,
Too aerial for grief:
Dead as the unstruck gong.

Long after twirl and spin,
Deleted, spare, and thin
In multiple retreat,

Feet rustle them. We rake
And burn them for the sake
Of dwelling in their smoke.

Oh kindle, day of days,
Unbroken blue in haze
The bitter burning sweet:
Sweet burning in our street.

What Am I Up To?

"I'll be right there," says the little man. Please note
He doesn't say "I'll be *left* there" — with his hat and coat.
"I'll be round soon," says the little man. He's thin as a rail.
"What am I in for?" he asks again, though he's not in jail.
"Will you help me out?" now he wants to know.
With a rope? A stepladder? With *what?*
                                        Hello!
"I'm coming down with measles," says the man's little son.
Oh, stay upstairs and have 'em, or come down with just one.

After Christmas

There were lots on the farm,
But the turkeys are gone.
They were gobbling alarm:
There were lots on the farm,
Did they come to some harm,
Like that poor little fawn?
There were lots on the farm,
But the turkeys are gone.

Just Because . . .

Kittens have paws they don't have pawses,
Lions have maws they don't have mawses,
Tigers have jaws they don't have jawses,
And crows have caws they don't have cawses.

I make one pause, I make two pauses:

Nine jackdaws aren't nine jackdawses,
Seven seesaws aren't seven seesawses,
Five oh pshaws aren't five oh pshawses,
Three heehaws aren't three heehawses.

Do you give two straws? Do you give two strawses?

A Christmas Package:
Nine Poems

1

I hung up a stocking —
A big one too:
Bigger than ever went
Into my shoe.
I knew all about
What I hoped would go in:
A ball in the heel
And the feel of a thin
Sort of ruler I've needed
For measuring things;
A long leash for Sokko,
My dog; the small wings
Of the folded-back part of
A glider I'll tie
With a towrope behind
Something else that will fly.
A flashlight, of course — for
You always get one;
And a reel for my rod,

Or a compass. The fun
Of a stocking is finding
You never quite get
What you counted on; somehow
You almost can bet
That the stuff you will feel —
All the bulges, those sharp
Little points — lack the shape
Of a reel for a carp.
They are more like an egg
With three joints, or the sag
Of corn muffins stuffed in
The south end of a bag.
And even the tube
Doesn't really quite flare:
It's no flashlight. And if
There's a glider in there,
You're my grandmother's uncle.
But *I'll* tell you what
I found stuffed in my stocking . . .
Gee whiz, no! I've got
To be getting on home;
But tomorrow, let's say,
You might like to swap
Me. If not, it's okay.

2

Here's that little girl who wraps each gift
with the same artistry and care she uses
dressing for a party: the same lift
of spirit, pondering as she chooses
color of paper, kind of ribbon or string,
striving to angle the folds at either end
to look professional as anything;
finding the made-for-it box to send
it off by mail — oh, in plenty of time
for Christmas — knowing (alas) too well
the recipient will commit the crime
of tearing it open as one cracks the shell
of a peanut, or rips the fancy cover
off chewing gum, off (say) a candy bar.
Nor will this child in all her life discover
where the true gift appreciators are.

3

Asked for another name for Santa Claus,
Some people say Kriss *Kingle* — perhaps because
The *Kingle* sounds like *king*. Well, that is wrong.
Kriss *Kringle*'s been the guy's name all along.

4

Rock candy: hard sweet crystals on a string:
Enough to break your teeth. A turkey wing
Does not prepare you for this sort of thing.

5

Alert, live reindeer galloping on air,
Those unsupported runners, and a fair-
Sized load inside old Santa's sleigh to boot:
Some shake their heads, and some don't give a hoot.

6

Though holly halos hang from many a nail,
These pine spruce balsam hemlock ones prevail,
Adorning doors till March! Them I bewail.

7

That broken star
at the top of the tree:
how broken can
an old star be?
Some other ornaments are cracked,
the tinsel's tarnished, and I think
the tree's too small. Twelve lights go on,
ten don't. They used to blink.

8

My stocking's where
He'll see it — there!
One-half a pair.

The tree is sprayed,
My prayers are prayed,
My wants are weighed.

I've made a list
Of what he missed
Last year. I've kissed

My father, mother,
Sister, brother;
I've done those other

Things I should
And would and could.
So far, so good.

9

A collar for Sokko,
The dog; for the cat,
What cats always get —
But who cares about that?
A birdbath for Trillo.
Who she? The canary.
The goat gets some stuff
For his smell that Aunt Mary
Can't stand — what she *can't* stand's
The smell of the goat.
Merry Christmas! How *are* you?
I've got a sore throat.

Now Say Good Night

Now say Good Night
they say Now say Good
Night O.K. I say all right
I'll say Good Nights all day
for spite I say I might
Why *Good?* What's Good
about it? Good? I doubt it
Light is better than Night good
or bad all bright the world
the sight of birds in flight
of winter snowy white Now
say good good good good good
night good night good night
good sleepy tight sleep tight
Now say Good Night

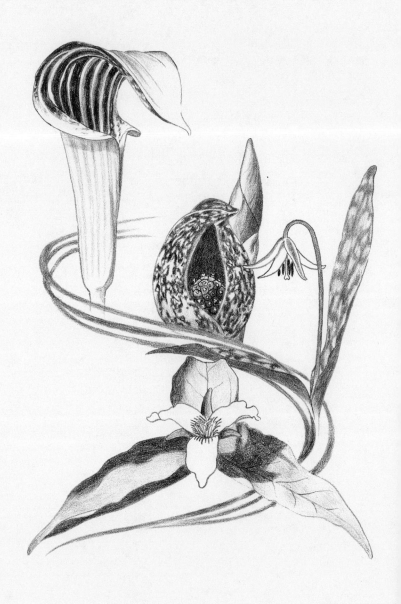

246

Spring Talk

Jack-in-the-pulpit: Where are you, Jack?
"He's out for a minute; he'll be right back."
Did you hear that? Real pulpit talk:
You hear it only the first spring walk.

Hello, skunk cabbage! Where's old skunk?
"He's rolled up here in the upper bunk."
Of course he isn't — he can't be. Who
Ever heard of a cabbage with bunks for two?

Well, dogtooth violet, and how's that tooth?
"It aches a bit, to tell the truth."
Now you heard *that:* he says it aches.
Let's ask wake-robin when robin wakes,

And toadstools where the toads have gone.
"They all went home. They leave at dawn.
Wake robin, though, and hear him sing."
Who wants to walk with me next spring?

Pad and Pencil

I drew a rabbit. John erased him
and not the dog I said had chased him.

I drew a bear on another page,
but John said, "Put him in a cage."

I drew some mice. John drew the cat
with nasty claws. The mice saw that.

I got them off the page real fast:
the things I draw don't *ever* last.

We drew a bird with one big wing:
he couldn't fly worth anything,

but sat there crumpled on a limb.
John's pencil did a job on *him*.

Three bats were next. I made them fly.
John smudged one out against the sky

above an owl he said could hoot.
He helped me with my wolf. The brute

had lots too long a tail, but we
concealed it all behind a tree.

By then I couldn't think of much
except to draw a rabbit hutch;

but since we had no rabbit now
I drew what must have been a cow,

with curvy horns stuck through the slats —
they both looked something like the bats.

And feeling sad about the bear
inside his cage, I saw just where

I'd draw the door to let him out.
And that's just all of it, about.

Innuendo

You are French? *Je suis.*
You speak French? *Mais oui.*
I don't speak French. *Non?*
I speak English. *Bon!*

All Day Long

Beneath the pine tree where I sat
to hear what I was looking at,

then by the sounding shore to find
some things the tide had left behind,

I thought about the hilltop blown
upon by all the winds I've known.

Why ask for any better song
in all the wide world all day long?

Lizette

"He knows my name." Lizette is five,
the boy who knows it, seven.
The bees bring honey to the hive,
but sweeter this girl's heaven
when the new boy by accident
had thrown his ball across
her fence. She, seeing where it went,
returned it with one toss.
He goes to school; she doesn't yet.
"Gee, whiz!" he said.
"Gee, whiz, Lizette!"

When Monkeys Eat Bananas

When monkeys eat bananas, these
Are monkeys in the zoos or zees.
We get these things all jungled up,
The way chicks have the pip or pup.
For monkeys swinging twos by twos
In threetops not in zees or zoos
Don't have bananas bad for teeth,
But luts of nots below beneath.

Mobile

Our little mobile hangs and swings
And likes a draft and drafty things:

Half-open doors; wide-window breeze,
All people when they cough or sneeze;

Hot dishes giving off their heat;
Big barking dogs, small running feet.

Our mobile's red and made to look
Like fish about to bite a hook:

Six fishes with a hook in front
Of each. They range in size — the runt,

Or baby, up to papa fish,
With hooks to match and make them wish

That they could reach the nice blue worms
A-dangle there with swirly squirms;

Six fishy mouths all open wide,
Six sets of teeth all sharp inside,

Six fishy holes where eyes should be,
Six fish to swim an airy sea.

I'm eating breakfast now, and they
Are watching me. And I must say

That every time I take a bite
I see and feel their sorry plight.

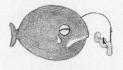

The Adventure of Chris

Chris met a toad.
"Hello," said Chris.
"Hello," said the toad,
"that's quite a load
of books you've got."
"See this?" said Chris,
who was thirsty and hot.
"It's Geography —
for telling me
what not to miss
on Earth."

Toad said,
"Does it say not to miss
the flower bed?
Or the edge of the pond?
Or across-lots what's
out back beyond?
Things under things —
like slimy slugs, like
bugs with wings?"

"No; but see this thick
Arithmetic
on how to divide,

subtract, and stuff?"

Toad said with pride,
"I eat things alive,
undivided. I've
been known to stuff —
yes, if there's enough.
I never subtract —
not *ever*. In fact,
my math isn't hard:
like how many hops
to the foot round the yard,
not counting the stops."

"Then there's spelling," said Chris,
who was tired of all this.

"That's for me, sure," said Toad.
"With the garden well hoed,
and the grass newly mowed,
and a good rainy spell.
Would your spelling book tell
about spells like that?"

"No!"

Well that's what the fat
talky toad said to Chris;
so let's end it on this.

The Clouds

All my life, I guess, I've loved the clouds.
I know some people as I don't know crowds.

Crowds swallow me. I lose myself and feel
that I am someone else, or else not real.

But clouds are not like people: as they pass,
I can know two or three, or such a mass

of flying clouds as fill the summer sky
and lose themselves; for always sailing by

are others just as good, and much the same
for being different. Clouds are like a game

that I don't seem to have to understand,
played without rules, with no one in command;

or like a picture puzzle on the go,
not asking to be solved by me below.

Clouds comfort me, and in such endless grace
I'm never lost and never lose my place.

The cool grey clouds at dawn devise the sea
in perfect stillness: just the beach and me.

Those thunderheads that pile above the sun,
so white before they blacken and I run,

are more than castles, mountains, what you will —
they're all my windows opening, opening still.

The farmer's and the seaman's clouds are plain
bone mackerels that swim before the rain.

I like them just because they serve to warn,
as when in fog the fogman blows his horn;

so puffy clouds that underlie one dread
dark canvas mean a hurricane ahead.

I like slow clouds that slide across the moon:
the long black arrows aimed to reach there soon.

The northern sky: St. Lawrence, the Great Lakes,
is where the west wind over water shakes

the sails of cloudy clipper ships that fill
with cumulus my skylight sill to sill.

All sunset clouds have color and that's when
I look for shape: a shark, a dragon's den,

a spouting whale, a giant, some great bird
or animal of which I've never heard.

I favor clouds that bring a solid fall
of fat wet Christmas flakes of snow; and all

the shower clouds of April come and gone;
big clouds that drag their shadows on the lawn,

or sweep their shadows from the mountain face —
all clouds, all seasons, sizes, any place.

Ten Twice

I say to you just so:
I know you think I think I know I know.
You say to me and I let it sink:
You know I think you think I think you think.

Bridges

The little bridge goes hop-across,
The big one humps his back;
The long one's half a spider web,
The flat one has a track.

The little bridge says, "See my fish";
The big one, "See my river";
The long one says, "See *me!* See *me!*"
The flat one starts to quiver

As you would, too, beneath a train.
The drawbridge says, "Well, I
Am going up for one good squint
About me in the sky."

I know them all: the long one scares,
The drawbridge makes you wait;
The big one dizzies me; I like
The flat one for the freight

That rumbles all its hundred cars
And heads for somewhere west;
But when I'm in the country . . .
Yes, I guess I know you've guessed:

That little bridge of hop-across
Keeps after me to stop.
I watch the wavy fish and see
My face, and maybe drop

A pebble in, or throw a small
Red berry down just right
To float above his fish; he
Doesn't say his fish will bite.

Rapid Reading

"A course in Rabbit Reading?"

"That's what she said. And something else like 'Addled Education.' "

"Rabbits? They can't read. You *know* they can't."

"The one in *Alice* could. At least he had a watch and told the time. And on the front door of his little house — remember? — there was a bright brass plate with W. RAB-BIT on it. I guess he could read *that*. Perhaps he couldn't spell out WHITE. Which shows . . ."

"*Alice* is a book. Look: Rabbits just don't read. They *breed*. She must have said 'Of course, in rabbit breeding . . .' "

"She didn't, though. She said *a* course in *Rabbit Reading*. Why? We haven't any rabbits that I know of."

"You should have asked her."

"She was on the phone with Mrs. Marples. She's still there on the phone with Mrs. Marples. I also heard her say 'Well lettuce, by all means.' What's *addled* anyway?"

"Just nuts, you nut. But *lettuce?* Did she laugh?"

"No."

"Gee, that's funny."

Balloons

(for Elise and Kate Mazzetti)

Kate's on for two, Elise is three,
They've been to the fair, as you can see,
for two balloons are sailing free.

They don't sail very high. They rise
from hands still pretty small in size
that held the strings. The face and eyes

on each balloon, as at the fair,
are looking toward the children there
below them as they take the air,

plumb full of gas. The steady tug
is upward. Gathered on the rug
are toys on wheels and dolls to hug.

The ceiling is the sky. It's white,
not blue. The strings within the tight
ten fingers slipped. The ceiling's height

is such Elise just can't quite reach
the string-end dangling down from each
balloon. But Kate's round eyes beseech

her: Stretch, oh, stretch your hand, Elise!
Tears follow. The balloons at ease
up yonder feel no wandering breeze

to move them. So they bob and bow,
their wide mouths smiling; but somehow
Elise *does* think it out. And now

we see her standing on a book.
She manages at last to crook
a finger round one string; and look!

she's giving it to Kate who sort
of likes this newest indoor sport.
Well, that's the end of my report.

Flicker

Up the road ahead
Flick goes a flicker;
Where the eye is quick
The bird is quicker.
Let the day hold still
So in his haste I hear
wick-whickering of wings
To please my ear.
Above his target tail
A white spot till he's gone
leaves but the chalk-like trail
To follow on
With eye if not with feet.
One feather of his
Floats down. How neat
And yellow it is.

Lemonade

It's lemonading time again:
Some take it sugary, some plain.
"Some take it the way I make it." Jane
Says that, and surely Jane should know,
For though it's noon and business slow,
She tends her shady roadside stand,

Both Greg and John prepared to hand
Each customer a cloudy glass
Of what might almost nearly pass
For lemonade. "Five cents a peg,
Or two for ten. I've change," says Greg:
Five nickels from his piggy-bank,
A dime from each for what they drank
Themselves before they opened shop
And watered down the pitchered pop.

What Are Pockets For?

What are pockets for?
An old piece of sash cord,
a knob from a door;
a small U magnet,
if you can find it;
a sprung clock spring,
with the key to wind it;
oodles of marbles,
a twist of copper wire;
a baseball calendar,
a flint for fire;
one soiled jack of hearts
or the five of spades;
that unshown copy of
your last month's grades;
two colored pebbles,
one hickory nut;
a shell, some fish line
with three feet of gut;
a cog out of something
which never did run;
a cellophane of candy —
I'll give you one;

your first circus ticket stub,
the snap you took
of the clown on the slack
wire before it shook;
a flashlight bulb,
a dirty green stamp;
the long-missing part of
your bicycle lamp;
one thin pair of pliers
to ply or to nip;
one old zipper fastener
with nothing to zip;
that half-busted harness-
bell you found inside
the barn on the farm,
and the buckle too wide
for its three-inch strap;
and a whole lot more
of stuff. Did you say,
What are pockets for?

October Wind

There is a sudden little wind that grieves
along the grounded edge of autumn leaves;

there is one even suddener that spreads
a lace of leaves on lawn and flower beds;

and there's a third not ever known to tire
of whirling piled-up leaves in flameless fire

the day before real burning can begin.
If someone says "Go back and rake them in,"

all through the gathered gold you'll hear that sad
small sudden wind just asking why you had

to make such piles unless it was for play.
And is that why you jumped in them today?

Frog in a Bog

Log, bog, and frog
All go together.
The *clementest* weather
(You guessed: the *best*)
For any frog isn't fog.
Give him hot bright sun —
A June one, an August one,
Or any of July's.
Flies are his prize:
Any kind, any size.
He is all eyes for flies.
A frog'll boggle
Up through scud of mud
So he can goggle
From the sedgy edge
Of grasses; or surprise,
Out of delicious skies,
Such wayward wings
Of things that may be had
Just as they tilt and skim
The dry green rim
Of lily pad.

Frog's a queer bloke
To hear him croak;
Queerer still in looks;
Queer leaper into brooks
Or ponds. We swim
Like him, not like a fish,
For he's our dish.
Real frogmen ape his style —
Though we don't see *them* smile.
His wide lips thin
Along his wider grin,
Dive in,
they seem to say,
OK,
Dive in.

Ducks Walking

Actually five,
if you count them twice,
just to see what it makes,
plus a couple of drakes
ducks trail in single file
with, man alive! *what* style!
Each drake of course has a nice
up-curving come-on feather
to his tail in any weather.
All seven, then,
perfection when
they bicycle round the pond.
No bicycle seat? I watch their feet.
But now, right here beyond
the dilly dream of open water,
just two drakes,
four feral ducks,
and someone's waddly
half-grown daughter.

Away and Ago

has the sound of over
the hills and far
away, but the rover
hasn't returned yet
for telling us what
it was that he met
with, or whether he got
there at all, or indeed
where it was that he chanced
to be choosing. So, losing
no time, I've advanced
out ahead of him,
standing or sitting so still
my away and ago lay
just over one hill
and not very distant.
I hope that you'll mind
not to follow too close,
not to fall far behind.

Says Tom to Me

Says Tom to me: "I slept the sleep of the just."
"An unjust thing *that* is for a boy like you!
You must have sleep — of course you *must*.
But without it, what did the just man do?"

The Walnut Tree

There was once a swing in a walnut tree,
As tall as double a swing might be,
At the edge of the hill where the branches spread
So it swung the valley right under me;
Then down and back as the valley fled.
I wonder if that old tree is dead?

I could look straight up in the lifting heart
Of the black old walnut there and start
My flying journey from green to blue
With a wish and a half that the ropes would part
And sail me out on a course as true
As the crows in a flock had dared me to.

I swung from the past to the far dim days
Forever ahead of me. Through the haze
I saw the steeple, a flash of white,
And I gave it a shout for the scare and praise
Of being a boy on the verge of flight.
And I pumped on the swing with all my might

Till the valley widened. Oh, I could guess
From the backward No to the forward Yes
That the world begins in the sweep of eye,
With the wonder of all of it more or less
In the last hello and the first goodbye.
And a swing in the walnut tree is why.

Mr. Spade and Mr. Pail

Mr. Spade and Mr. Pail and Mr. Henry Digger,
The three of them, the beach and sun,
The big world growing bigger
As Mr. Spade in Henry's hands
Selects the special kind of sands
That Mr. Pail is made to hold:
Not creamy white or golden gold,
But something super which the sea
Has left for Mr. Henry D.
With which to have his fun.

Now Mr. Pail is fairly full, and Mr. Henry Digger
Has said to Mr. Spade, "I wish
That Mr. Pail were bigger."
But Mr. Pail has just replied
That he is big enough inside;
For after all, when one is filled
And hopping hops, if sand is spilled,
Why then it's up to Mr. Spade
To fix the mess the sand has made.
"But if you catch a fish,"

Says Mr. Spade to Mr. Pail and Mr. Henry Digger,
"You'll need some water. Sand won't do,
And though I might be bigger,
No water ever sticks to *me* —
Not all the water in the sea.
You'd better have me dig a hole,
Then dig a ditch. The sea will roll
Right in, all frothy at the lip,
And Mr. Pail won't mind the dip;
The fish will like it too."

Now Mr. Spade and Mr. Pail — *not* Mr. Henry Digger —
The twain of them are lying where
The sea is growing bigger.
The tide is coming in quite fast,
But Mr. Digger couldn't last
At digging. He has gone to help
Himself to strings of stranded kelp;
So Mr. Pail and Mr. Spade
Are done for if he doesn't wade.
Does no one really care

For Mr. Spade and Mr. Pail? Not even Mr. Digger
Has seen them floating out and how

The waves are breaking bigger,
While Mr. Spade in Mr. Pail
Is saying "Have you hoisted sail?"
And Mr. Pail is saying "No.
I guess perhaps we'd better, though."
But Mr. Spade replies "I think
It might be wiser just to sink;
In fact, we're sinking now."

Oh, Mr. Spade! Oh, Mr. Pail! remember Mr. Digger
While you are restive in your grave —
A grave that's growing bigger.
But don't forget as tides run out
How very soon they turn about.
Yes, you will find yourselves once more,
I'm glad to tell you, on the shore.
"I hear a voice," says Mr. Pail;
"A fish, perhaps, or else a whale;
Or could it be our brave

Young lad — where *are* you, Mr. Spade? — our
      brave young Henry Digger?"
It couldn't, I regret to say;

It might, if he were bigger.
The morrow morning on the beach,
Half buried in the sandy reach,
Lies Mr. Pail with battered face.
Of Mr. Spade not any trace
Until a bather, crying "Oh!"
Has stepped on what I guess you know . . .
Where's Henry, anyway?

Pumpkins

October sun for miles and miles and miles;
and we were passing piles and piles and piles
of pumpkins — pumpkin-like, so like each other
no pumpkin knew one pumpkin from his brother.
If they were carved and placed in aisles and aisles,
with piles and piles of smiles and smiles and smiles
for miles and miles and miles on some dark night,
and one could handle, candle them, and light
the whole creation with Jack Pumpkinheads,
they'd be no wiser. What a pumpkin dreads
is being so conspicuous with eyes
and nose and mouth. Much better off in pies,
say pumpkins. So for miles and miles and miles,
with piles of pumpkins — aisles and aisles of piles —
just putting all their pumpkinheads together,
you couldn't tell what they were thinking: whether
they thought of Halloween, or where they grew
in yellow pumpkin fields. I'd say the view
was pleasing to those pumpkins at the top —
which were of course the best ones in the crop.
But since they had no eyes nowise to know,
they might as well have been down there below;
nor could they guess that mile on mile on mile
some boy was hoping he might see one smile.

Figures of Speech

"Now come to think of it," you say.
I'll come, of course. Come where?

"High time you're up!" *High* time? How high?
Both clock-hands in the air?

You had "a high old time"? I'm glad.
Why *old*, though? Weren't you there?

A Word or Two on Levinia

Levinia was a simple child, to whom words meant just
    what they said:
"To meet a deadline," she supposed, meant meet a
    lion dead.
"Nice boy, of course; but there is really nothing in his
    head"

Concerned Levinia — Harold's head was like a tennis
    ball?
All hollow? Well, he never seemed to bounce when he
    would fall.
"Think twice," they say. How can you, if you haven't
    thought at all?

"I simply don't see through it," said somebody on the
    phone.
What was somebody thinking of? The wall? The door?
    A stone?
What is an "own" when people say they'll "do it on
    their own"?

Levinia's father once remarked, "The whole thing has
    been swept
Under the rug." Which rug? And would the thing be
    squashed if stepped

On? Father didn't help. He said the whole thing
would be kept

A secret. As to secrets, one which baffles that small Miss
Is something overheard today. It seems her Uncle
Bliss
Said, "They will come out of the woodwork if they
ever hear of this!"

The Cellar Hole

Between our house and Jack's next door
They dug a cellar long before

Bulldozers were invented. Men
Used picks and spades and dug, and when

They'd dug a big hole three or two
Feet deep that Friday, they were through

Till Monday. Friday night the rain
Came down all night, and it was plain

Not Saturday would stop it, nor
Would Sunday, when it rained some more.

On Monday noon it stopped while we
Were both in school; but after three,

When Jack and I ran home, we found
A pond with no one else around,

And got our rubber boots and stuff.
The month was May, and warm enough.

Jack's steamboat took a while to heat
The boiler, but I had a fleet

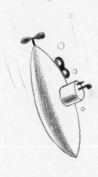

Of sailboats going, and my sub
I'd got for Christmas. In the tub

It wasn't much, but now it dived
Right down. Then other kids arrived

With boots and boats and stuff and made
An awful splash. They couldn't wade

Unless they yelled. Their yells were loud,
And pretty soon we had a crowd

Of kids with boots, young brats with boats.
"If we could make a raft that floats,"

Said Johnny, and I said, "Why not
With these three planks?" We sank a lot

Of kids whose boats wound up with keys,
And they wound up by losing these.

Jack had his steamboat going now;
But just as he was showing how

To set the rudder, something broke,
And someone gave the thing a poke,

So round it circled, tooting toots
Just as I filled my rubber boots

With fresh mud-water; but by then
They didn't need it. That was when

Poor Jerry came. He had no luck.
He had no boat. He brought a duck.

A lot of good that did for him:
It didn't want to stay and swim.

Next day they spaded up my sub.
It never worked well in the tub.

Boo Moo

Cats and owls
see better than fowls?
Ducks and pigs
sing better in wigs?
One is false, one partly true.
Perhaps you think the cow says *Moo?*
In Webster's Dictionary, *Boo!*
Just look it up: I ask you to.
Then ask the cow, and I am through.

I'm pretty well, myself. How you?

Young Sammy

Young Sammy, when he was no more
than — maybe less than — yes, than four,
had trouble with the names of things
that walk or swim or fly with wings.
He'd never tell you those are cows.
"See, Sammy? What are those?" "Those clows,"
he'd answer. Chickens in their coop
looked more like jiggins. He would whoop
delight to see a flock of birds,
or — if you understood him — virds.
A turtle, sunning on a log,
to him was turkle; and a frog
became a flog when Sammy spoke
about him. Why not? Flogs can cloak
as frogs cannot; and so his vat
vlew vaster than a tumbly bat.
His rabbits weren't, his labbits were;
his clitten, like the clat, had vur;
the pond was full of pickerel —
too long a word; particural
when there were frogs in it, and tads —

he said that right — and lilyplads
above which sailed the waggonvlies
like whirlybirds cut down to size.
But Sammy now is six and knows
a flog's a frog. If "What are those?"
he says to *you*, your zoo reply
is pachyderms or platypi.

Like You As It

Don't write *alright* — that's wrong!
All right — two words. OK?
No, *not* "Just like you say."
If anything, that's wronger!
Why "Like you say?" *Like's* longer
than *as* is — twice as long.
To use *like* in that way —
   "Like in a field of hay,"
   "Like Johnny said today,"
   "Like if the Sox don't play,"
   "Like when the clock goes *Bong!*"
Wrong, wrong, wrong — Chinese *Wong* —
gosh-awful, fierce, bizarre!
I listen, hear, and see
how ignorant you are:
your mental age is three,
if you think "Like you say"
is right. It isn't. Now
try *"As* you say." See how
much better *that* sounds? Try

"*As* in a field of hay,"
"*As* Johnny said today,"
"Say *if* the Sox don't play,"
"*As* when the clock goes *Bong!*"
All right. You stretch a thong
and bend your bow to shoot
your arrows *as* you should —
out straight for keeps. For good.
And *don't* let some galoot
who likes *like — as he will —*
some Tom, Dick, Harry, Bill,
who doesn't give a hoot,
punch AS right on the snoot!

Bumblebee

The bumblebee is bumbly,
acting anything but humbly.
Into flowers he's a tumbler
all day long — a bandit bumbler.
Does his buzzing mean *Beg pardon!*
as he zooms about the garden?
No. And so, if you were roses,
would you want him rubbing noses?
And about that drop of honey:
would *you* sell it for no money?
No again. But bee's to blossom
what persimmon is to possum.

Bumblebee, with yellow sweater,
though you haven't won your letter,
I can see your legs all chappy
like a cowboy's. You're not happy
like a cowboy. No, sir, stranger!
And you pack a lot more danger.
You don't ride the range just singing.
You've got wings. When they're not winging,

I observe that you don't fold 'em.
Honey bees do that. You hold 'em
up. Hold up your flowers, too;
but please don't ever . . .

                              you know who!

Dr. Ping and Mr. Pong

Said Dr. Ping to Mr. Pong:
"I'll tell you what you do that's wrong."
"I didn't know I do a thing
That's wrong," said Pong to Dr. Ping.
"You drive the ball so hard — so *much*
Too hard! That's why it doesn't touch
The table. If you'll save an ounce
Of strength, the ball will touch and bounce.
OK? You never serve an ace?
Well, roll the ball across the face
Of your flat paddle, *in between*
Your palm and it. You've never seen
So fast a spin," said Dr. Ping.
"But just be sure you always swing
Your paddle through a graceful arc.
No Mickey Mantle in the park
Can throw a ball like what you'll get
In skimming it across the net."
"I see," said Pong to Ping. "But, Doc,
Although you started in to knock
My game, I say your backhand's weak.
But let that pass. If I may speak
Quite frankly, it's your lob you need
To work on. Why stand there and feed
Opponents what they'll smash right back?

A tricky lob is what you lack."
This so unsettled Dr. Ping,
That he and Pong are practicing.
They hardly ever *play* the game
To which each somehow gave his name.

OZ

Is Oz?
Oz was.
I knew it well.
Is Oz?
Dear Land! It cast a spell
on me that I'm not over yet.
Can you imagine I'd forget
the Wizard? Could my mind erase
Tin Woodman, Dorothy? Misplace
Jack Pumpkinhead, the Scarecrow, Tip?
The Saw-Horse, Gump, Billina? Skip
the Cowardly Lion? I guess not!
Would Tiktok tick if one forgot
the Nome King? What would Scarecrow do
to me if I'd not tell you who
was H. M. Woggle-Bug, T.E.?
His letters still spell THEM to me.
THEM isn't all that they imply:
H.M.T.E. *is* THEM, though. Try
H(2) M(4) T(1) and E,
you'll find, just must be — oh, yes, (3).

And then there's Ozma who, of course,
was — that's a secret. Funny! Force
of habit makes me say these things.
The Wheelers? Did they fly with wings?
They rolled on wheels. The Scoodlers? Should
I blurt out *everything?* I could.
This Ozman (which I am) still keeps
his hat on even while he sleeps,
for who can say in Oz what's next?
It doesn't do to tax the text.
Just keep on going, book through book:
In Oz you see before you look.
In Oz you wake before you dream,
in Oz you're never what you seem,
in Oz you do before you dare.
In Oz — but maybe you've been there?
A lot of people have, I guess.
Is Oz then? Yes, yes, three times yes!
Is Oz?
You *know* it is, don't you?
I hoped you did.
I thought you do.

Corinna

Dinner!
Where's Corinna?
Dinner!
Where's Corinner?
Where's Corinner? Innerout?
Corinner risout, no doubt.
Corinner! *Dinner!*
Hearer shout?
And now Corinner resin
from wherever Corinner rasbin.
Corinner reatser dinner
at last — and fast:
most of it sinner.

Ants and Sailboats

I ate my sandwich on the rocks.
The racing boats were out at sea,
All white and misty, and the docks
Across the harbor looked at me.

An ant came by. I scattered crumbs,
Some big ones, mostly from the crust.
The sails stuck up like tiny thumbs
And fingernails. I guess I must

Have watched ten minutes while they spread
Or stacked themselves like cards to bunch
Beyond the islands; and I fed
Myself the peach and finished lunch.

From time to time I watched the ant:
He circled round as he'd refuse
One crumb and then another. Can't
Make up his mind which one to choose,

I thought; and then a bigger red
And bully ant came up and they
Compared antennae. Which one fled?
The red one. When he ran away

Some other black ones zagged across
The rock face. Each one seemed to know
The others, but if one was boss,
I couldn't tell. The sails stood low

Against the sky; but ants move fast.
And pretty soon one got his nips
On such a crumb as made a vast
Unwieldy burden. All the ships

And sails out quartered on the breeze
Were nothing to this active race
Of people shouldering with ease
Their weight, and then some, over space

Of rock and making off for where
They had their crevice home. It could
Have been a long way. Time to spare
Was not for them. This ant was good

At pushing his selection straight
Ahead of him until he came
To obstacles — though not so great
He couldn't pull it over. Game

And solid efforts dragged it up
Each thimble mountain, over straws
Like logs to him, till in the cup
Of one green leaf he seemed to pause,

Then left the crumb and ran for help
Or haven. Fringy grass hung down
Above the rocks where withered kelp
Concealed his passage home to town.

Would he remember where he hid
His food? I looked my last on sails.
Or was it that he never did
Admit himself an ant who fails?

Ptarmigan

O Ptarmigan, O ptarmigan,
O ptarmigan: pt
is such a funny way to start

a name. Don't you agree?
You've never had pneumonia,
though you live among the Lapps
and Eskimos inhabiting
those ice-cold ptops of maps.
There's no one here to ptell me
how you ptolerate that name!
It saddens me to think that
someone like me was to blame.
Some ancient Gael? It wasn't. No,
his word was *tārmachan.*
The Greek for feather? *pteron;* but
did Greeks know how you fan
your feathered feet to walk on snow?
You wouldn't walk on ptar;
and, anyway, the Greeks live south
and never got that far.
Some day, I guess, I'll travel north
and ask a caribou
or reindeer: How's your pterritory?
Got a Pt-V ptoo?

Four Little Ducks

One little duck
In a pond is ducky:
A duck with luck.
Then lucky lucky

Two little ducks
And the pond grows duckier;
Three little ducks
And the ducks' luck luckier.

Four little ducks
Set the big geese hissing.
The old hen clucks
"Four ducks are missing!"

"Four little ducklings,"
Geese tell gander.
Curious clucklings:
Old hen *and* her

Chicks (cheep cheep)
Begin to chorus,
"Ducks! (peep peep)
In the pond before us."

The ducklings quack
Quacks high and thready:
"We won't come back
Until we're ready."

"And when will *that* be?
When? O *when?*"
"O geese O gee!
O when O hen!"

"Fresh young quackers,
Don't you think?"
"Wisecrack crackers!
Let them sink."

The geese hiss hisses,
Hen clucks clucks
With hits and misses
At those young ducks.

The ducklings quack quack
Back: "Don't meddle!"
They jibe and tack
(They really pedal);

The quacklings duck
(They're upside down);
Perhaps they're stuck,
Perhaps they'll drown;

Perhaps they'll not,
Perhaps they won't;
They know a lot.
Don't think they don't.

Four little webby
Pinkfoot truants;
It's just well mebbe
They lack influence

And don't know how
Much risk is risky.
A turtle, now,
Could snap one frisky

Foolish swimmer.
They have no mom.
Their chance grows dimmer
As they grow calm.

A turtle big
And round and flat?
The ducks don't dig
A thing like that.

A shadow glides
Up from the mud
Toward undersides
Of flesh and blood.

Old Snap's sharp eye
Has seen them pass.
The pedals fly:
They swim on glass.

Which yellow sailor
Will turtle take?
The geese grow paler,
The chicks all shake.

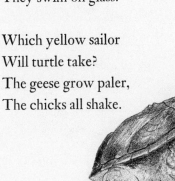

317

"Look out! Look *out!*"
The geese give warning.
But geese can't shout.
Well, just this morning,

To round them up
Is a boy out rowing.
His dog's no pup:
A wise old knowing

Red retriever,
Name of Thor,
A firm believer
In ducks ashore.

His mouth drools drooly,
Soft and quick;
He does things coolly,
Knows each trick

And duckly skitter:
All old hat
To Thor, more fitter
Than any cat.

He's poised and ready
With big-dog splash!
He's swimming steady
While ducklings dash,

Till one gets caught
And two get caughter,
As three well ought
And four well oughter.

One says, "Yes,"
The second, "Yessir!"
The pond grows less
And less and lesser

Full of flighty
Ducklings. Thor
Gives one good mighty
Shake, once more

Inside the boat.
The big drops shaken
From his red coat,
The unforsaken

Fluffy clutch
Of ducks together
Quack — as much
To say "What weather!"

Geese stop hissing,
Hen-clucks cease.
There's not one missing.
All is peace.

In pondy muck
For Snap no dinner.
No duck, no luck;
He's thin, he's thinner.

The days go by.
No duck appears.
Why magnify
My lack of tears?

Only

Only is a lonely little word,
used wrongly by so many. You have heard
a person say, "I *only* saw him twice";
which makes you wonder, Did they phone, write nice
long letters? Meaning that they knew
each other well? This isn't true.
"I saw him *only* twice" does still admit
that other phone-and-letter side of it.
So if that lonely *only*, modifying
saw, still seems just not quite satisfying,
then say, "My *only* knowledge of him was,
I saw him twice." That slams the door, it does!

Japanese Lesson

Take Haru, Natsu:
Japanese for Spring, Summer.
Now: *Aki? Fuyu?*

Two Times Three

In summer these —
they always come in threes:
    a spot of hot,
    a pool of cool,
        or else the breeze,
        not round my knees
but up the valley
        soft and light and high
        as bees in trees.

In winter those
three best for when it snows:
    desire of fire,
    of bed ahead —
        no frozen toes,
        dire nosey blows
while up the chimney
        soft and light and high
        smoke cozy goes.

Beech

I like the circling proud old family beech,
The carefully tailored cut of his grey bark;
His lower branches glad enough to reach
Straight out and touch the earth and leave no mark
Against the sky; the way his twigs turn up,
Like fingers of the hand, each barbel cup
Of gold from which will come the bronzy leaf.
His sails and topsails set without a reef,
All summer now he sways across the lawn;
And when from other trees the leaves are gone,
He furls the faded paper his became.
Some flutter dryly mentioning his name,
If you should find them there when only snow
Is on the ground where most leaves had to go.

O-U-G-H

(some thoughts, thowts, or thoots thereon)

This letter combination makes it tough
for people learning English. Who can bluff
his way, pronouncing *though*, *bough*, *cough*, and *sough*
as if, when he has finished, that's enough?

It isn't. He will find he's not quite *through*.
I'm glad we just spell *do* the way we do.
It might be *dough*. Why shouldn't *cough* be *coo?*
Sough's *suff*, but also *sow*. *Bough* might be *boo*.

Supposing *though*'s *not tho*, but more like *thoff*,
and *sough*'s *sow*'s not a pig that *sows*, but *soff?*
then pigs might eat from *truffs*, not from a *troff*.
and you'd mix cough-links up with cuffs that *coff*.

I bow to you; the bow-wow barks; a bow
shoots arrows, fixes ribbons. So we go,
since that pig's *trough* could very well be *trow*,
except that *trow*'s not just a rhyme for *flow:*

trow rhymes with *ow* as in an *Ouch!* I guess
that's all we'd better say about this mess.

Jamboree

A rhyme for ham? *Jam.*
A rhyme for mustard? *Custard.*
A rhyme for steak? *Cake.*
A rhyme for rice? *Another slice.*
A rhyme for stew? *You.*
A rhyme for mush? *Hush!*
A rhyme for prunes? *Goons.*
A rhyme for pie? *I.*
A rhyme for iced tea? *Me.*
For the pantry shelf? *Myself.*

Daybreak

Dawn? blinks Fawn.
What's going on?

Day! screams Jay:
Day, *Day* — Today!

That's so, caws Crow.
You didn't know?

Faint streak of light:
Check that, Bob White?

We see it: Squa-a-a-w-w-k!
(three Nighthawks talk).

Too loud, cries Cloud:
You boys too loud!

You want to wake
some sleepy Snake?

Or hear me sing?
chirps Chipperwing.

Amen to *that!*
squeaks Flit the Bat.

Amen to flittern,
too, booms Bittern.

I cease to prowl
at dawn, says Owl;

You mean you perch
on *me*, brags Birch.

In truth, in troth,
murmurmurs Moth

who likes it dark
in Birch's bark.

Sky's *really* grey
now. *Day!* screams Jay.

Yes. Take a look,
says Trout in Brook.

You see that Fly?
Well, so do I.

I'll leave this ring
where Swallows wing.

Day's night for Fox;
to heck with clocks!

All's night for Moles
like us in holes.

Me too! I surface,
though, says Shrew.

Get off my ground!
cracks Scamperound,

the Squirrel. *My* log!
pipes Lep, the Frog.

Crawl under, Bug,
with me — with Slug.

OK, says Tree:
not under me.

Not under *him?*
mocks Broken Limb,

that tough old Oak?
I'm glad I broke.

You used to toss
in wind, says Moss;

you're rotten wood
now — very good.

Don't leave *your* house,
I notice, Mouse!

He's scared of Cat,
whines Water Rat.

Who wouldn't be?
twits Phoebe. We

birds have a slew
of danger. You

folks hide at will;
we fly, sit still.

A lot of harm
there, round that farm;

not Cow, of course,
or Pig, or Horse;

but Cat and Shrike
and Hawk — suchlike.

The woods are best:
here's where we nest.

Peek in, now. *Hush!*
says Hermit Thrush.

No nest of mine,
pants Porcupine:

all woods are tough.
I've had enough.

Old noisy Quill:
Keep still! Keep still!

You! Silence now!
That Farmer's Cow?

Just sound of axe,
quacks Duck. Relax.

Drum . . . *Drum?* Just some
old Grouse's drum.

No! *No!* thumps Snow-
shoe Rabbit. *No!*

That's Silver Tongue:
Hot Dog! He's young.

But on the loose,
warns Wren. Vamoose!

Run, run! bangs Gun,
lest you be done.

Where? *Where?* grunts Bear,
who looks like Scare.

Here, answers Deer,
who leaps like Fear . . .

No, *no!* says Doe.
It can't be so . . .

on, on, with Fawn.
Why *must* it dawn?

Think! Think! No, slink
away like Mink.

Hide! Hide! some Groundhog
whistles. *Hide!*

O bunk! sniffs Skunk,
the one with spunk.

Mr. Mixup Tells a Story

Under the rabbit there, I saw a tree —
Well, you know what I mean.
His ears were green and leafy . . . you asked me
to *tell* you, didn't you, just what I'd seen?

Well, anyhow, out peered that big red box.
Red fox? Did I say *box?* A fox it was!
He didn't see me. I looked up my clocks . . .
My *watch?* My watch to watch how long he does.

How long he *took?* A nice word, *took.* That's right . . .
to spot my rabbit up above his spine —
his pine. No, rabbits don't have wings. It's quite
enough to wiggle nose. Can't wiggle mine.

Ten days went by. You say *ten minutes?* Why?
Because it happened yesterday? It should.
Then suddenly I saw the fellow fly.
Which fellow? Couldn't he? Oh, yes, he could.

And that old boxed-up wolf. I tell you he . . .
I don't know which direction. What's the diff?
He didn't catch — he wasn't after *me.*
What rabbit? Well, speak up! No matter if.

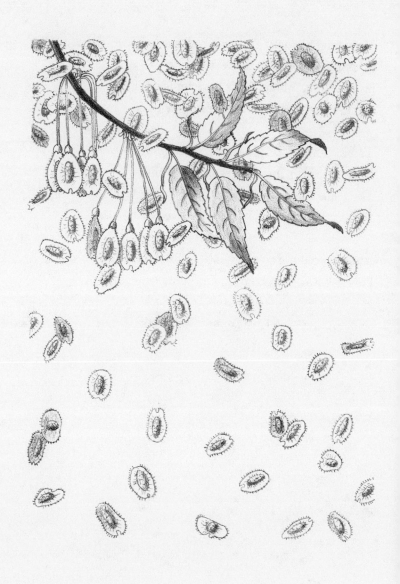

Elm Seed Blizzard

Along about then, the middle of May,
I say to myself: "any day . . ."
And I guess up there in the tall elm trees
The leaves say something like "Listen, breeze:
It's no good *whispering* stuff; just *blow!*
There's a skyful of seed here set to go."
And the breeze perks up
And the seeds fly loose —
Not hard like acorns, or cones like spruce —
But tiny saucers without a cup,
Till the air is full of their golden flutter
On street and sidewalk, lawn and gutter;
On windowsills, on doorsteps, mats;
On coats and pants and skirts and hats;
On people, dogs; in shoes, in cars;
On roller-skates, on handlebars;
On everything and everywhere;
Pale flakes of gold with piles to spare.

Well, a big wind comes and blows it all
Up down the street in a golden wall

To fill the air and fill your pockets
With billions out of a billion sockets:
Every saucer papery-thin:
One seed in the middle of each, sealed in.

If it happens to rain, then a cornflake slush,
Like a yellow boxtop cereal mush
Is under your feet, with a swirling flow
By the curbstone: squash, squash, squash, you go,
Till the cloggy mass that the sun dries out
Makes little gold islands all about.

You'd think, with all these seeds around,
A million elms would spring from the ground!
But nothing happens: the golden storm
Has gone like snow when the air gets warm:
Gone down the drain, gone up the sky,
Gone out with the cleaning trucks gone by —
Though somewhere, far away from me,
One lost blown seed becomes a tree.

Along about then, the middle of May,
I say to myself: "any day . . ."
I have only to say it. The trees let go,
And the air goes gold with a golden snow.

Trouble with Pies

Tomorrow's Christmas Day: three kinds of pies —
apple, mince, and pumpkin — all same size,
though not much bigger round than hungry eyes.

Since my first try at pie, I cannot choose
between mince, apple, pumpkin; or refuse
one, taking two of all those three good twos.

Apple and mince? Apple and pumpkin? What?
Leave pumpkin out, or mince? Well I guess not!
Pumpkin and mince? No apple have I got.

It would be better — best — to take all three;
but somehow that's not what they say to me.
"Which *do* you want?" they say. I say, "Let's see . . ."

Singular Indeed

One mouse adds up to many mice,
One louse adds up to lots of lice,
One chickenhouse to chickenhice.

The grouse — a noble bird! But *grice!*
What would you feed *them* — rouse or rice?
Or some old slouse of bread, or slice?

Take tub — you take it. Like to souse?
Or sice? One cold as ouse or ice
Is not so nouse, is not so nice.

Books Fall Open

Books fall open,
you fall in,
delighted where
you've never been;
hear voices not once
heard before,
reach world on world
through door on door;
find unexpected
keys to things
locked up beyond
imaginings.
What *might* you be,
perhaps *become*,
because one book
is somewhere? Some
wise delver into
wisdom, wit,
and wherewithal
has written it.

True books will venture,
dare you out,
whisper secrets,
maybe shout
across the gloom
to you in need,
who hanker for
a book to read.

Ivory

A cake of soap, a toothpick mast,
a paper sail, ahoy, avast,
and other sloopy sounds, and John
is in the bath with nothing on.

He wastes a lot of soap each tub
he takes, but he's not one to scrub;
and soapboats do the sudsing while
the boy is sailing up the Nile.

The White Nile's full of *sudd* — a word
(two d's) of which too few have heard:
some vegetable stuff that floats
and fills the river, stops the boats

from running up and down at will.
But John's boat isn't all that still.
His only problem, ever since
he made a boat, is when to rinse.

Knotholes

To make a knothole,
Knock out the knot;
And having a knothole,
What have you got?
You've got whatever
The fence shut in.
With lots of knots,
Where they have been
You've got whatever
The fence shut out.
You see what knotholes
Are all about?

Tom and Joe

Tom loves to be heard;
Joe not at all
Boom!
Can you hear Joe's small
voice? No? It seems to have died!
Boom!
You can hear *that*, though?
Yes? Well, *I told you so!*
I imply — I've implied;
You infer — you've inferred
that I'm *not* on Tom's side,
nor on Joe's. My one word
is: *Don't* be a Tom
who explodes like a bomb.
And oh, yes: on the other
hand, *Don't* be a Joe!

Mr. Macklin's Visitor

Mr. Macklin's back in town:
A light shines from his shed.
His face, you'll notice, yellow-brown —
Much like a pumpkin head.

Tomorrow night is Halloween:
No pumpkins, though, as yet
For him to carve. He must have seen
To it too late to get

Those special ones he never
Is without this time of year.
I can't remember ever
Having seen him look so drear,

Dismayed, distraught, defeated —
Something much like that. "Gee whiz!"
Thought Flip, who found him seated
By that toolhouse door of his.

Flip said, "Hello! What's wrong?" to
Mr. Macklin — slow, like that.
It didn't take him long to
Hear, "No pumpkins!" Whose black cat

Was this one slipping quickly
From the shed? Flip saw him plain
And felt his skin grow prickly.
Mr. Macklin said again:

"No pumpkins, Flip. Go take a
Look inside the shed. You'll see."
Flip took a look. You'd quake a
Bit, had you to disagree

With Mr. Macklin, yelling
"You've got three fat pumpkins here,"
And Mr. Macklin telling
Him, "You're crazy!" Something queer

Has happened. What's that bristly
Old broom doing, lying there
On top of them? Sharp thistly
Voice of Mr. Macklin: "Where

Is my *new* broom? I bought it
Just today. It hung from that
Big nail." If Flip had thought it
Through, Well, what of that black cat?

And who (if Flip were thinking)
Swaps an old broom for a new?
Why, one who owns a slinking
Black cat. One by night who flew

On brooms. Three pumpkins? Three? Three
Stands for broom, for cat, for her.
Strange Mr. Macklin. *Does* he see?

"Which, Flip, do you prefer?"

November Bares the Robin's Nest

November bares the robin's nest
We had to part the leaves to see;
And even then we thought it best
To glance and go, and let it be.
The mother in another tree
Said "Don't you dare to touch those eggs!"
We never did. They hatched, and we
Thought: *What big mouths and what small legs.*

The fledglings fattened, feathered out;
The days grew long, mouths widened wide.
I guess the worms and bugs about
All vanished from the countryside.
How well the full green leaves could hide
Such dark digestion going on!
But then one day the youngsters tried
Their wings. Three days, and they were gone.

Bone-dry, the vacant nest shows up —
A shabby, tattered thing of straw
And stuff, so little like the cup
Of skyblue eggs that first we saw.
The rains have rotted it; the raw
Damp easterly has torn and frayed
The edges. On the branch, *caw-caw*,
The black crow settles and is swayed.

Wintry

Hylas in the spring,
Crickets in the fall:
In winter not a thing
To sing itself at all.

Fireflies follow May,
Bonfires Halloween;
Nothing lights up grey
Old winter in between.

Come Christmas

You see this Christmas tree all silver gold?
It stood out many winters in the cold,

with tinsel sometimes made of crystal ice,
say once a winter morning — maybe twice.

More often it was trimmed by fallen snow
so heavy that the branches bent, with no

one anywhere to see how wondrous is
the hand of God in that white world of his.

And if you think it lonely through the night
when Christmas trees in houses take the light,

remember how his hand put up one star
in this same sky so long ago afar.

All stars are hung so every Christmas tree
has one above it. Let's go out and see.

Forget It

I'm not too sure that all I've read
Is under my hat or over my head;
What I've forgotten, so far as I see,
Is a matter between myself and me.
If things remembered since I was young
I don't keep right on the tip of my tongue,
It doesn't mean *something* won't come out!
What is it you want to know about?

The Poultry Show

Who wants to go to the poultry show?
"I do," "I might," "I will."
Three fat ducks trip heel to toe:
webfoot, wipefoot, waddlefoot go
down from the round little man-made hill
to the man-made round little pond below.
A pair of bantam cocks beyond,
with stretched necks straining, can't outcrow
one Indian wyandotte whose legs
are feathered (the hens lay feathered eggs,
some say). What a hoe-down crow-down show!

This incubator company sells
you chicks sidestepping out of shells,
or pecking specks on the window glass,
and you will find it hard to pass
the wet ones getting dry.
                              You'll *never* pass them by!
They'll sell you brooders, so you can brood
those chicks whose manners are very rude.
Or you can buy fine poultry food —
cracked corn, oats, buckwheat, barley, bran.
And drinking fountains: a fancy can
that sits and slobbers in a pan.

These combs and wattles of big birds —
big *roosters*: careful of your words! —
add color to the rows and rows
and rows of noisy crowing. Shows
like this will make you wonder why
you ever ate that chicken pie,
or boiled an egg you might have tried
to hatch, if you had been supplied
a steady heat of one-naught-three
degrees three weeks. You'd have to be
alert to turn the warm eggs twice
a day. That thought itself is nice.

Right now you'll have to pause and tell
yourself about the poultry smell
of poultry shows. Some things are well
enough alone, just as they are:
Treat eggs as eggs; let chickens star,
win ribbons, have a fresh clean cage,
or otherwise they will engage
a lot more of your time than you
have got. You'd better think this through.

Please *don't* say that those roosters *crew*:
It's just the British ones that do.
They *crowed*. They do it in the dawn,
unless a poultry show is on.

I personally prefer to yawn.

Orion

Orion in the cold December sky
Looks out upon the earth, the leaves gone by,
Swings over church and steeple down the slack
Of starfields to the western gate out back.
I see his belt (three stars) the studding grace
Of giants striding up through stellar space
Indifferent to satellites and all
That man has made and rocketed. How tall
He stands! How glad I am to know
His name and shape. One wonders here, below
His range and region, why we do not dare
In sight of all the bounty earth can bear,
In loneliness of flesh and blood and bone,
To walk as steadfast, and to walk alone.

Laundromat

You'll find me in the Laundromat — just me and shirts and stuff:
Pajamas, pillowcases, socks and handkerchiefs enough.
I've put them in my special tub — the third one from the right,
And set the switch for *Warm*, and shoved the coin and got the light,
And sprinkled blue detergent on the water pouring in,
Closed down the lid and bought a Coke to watch the shakes begin
To travel up the line of empty units. How they show
Their pleasure just to feel one fellow full and on the go!
Well, now it's all one train: a nice long rumbly kind of freight,
Of which I am the engineer. We're running on the straight.
In Diesel Number Three I've got the throttle open wide,
And blow for every crossing through the pleasant countryside.
The light turns amber. Pretty soon some other washers bring
Their bulgy bags of clothes and make tubs nine and seven sing.
But nine and seven haven't got the squiggle, squash, and drive
Of Number Three. May sound alike to you, but I'm alive
To certain water music that the third one seems to make.
I hear it change from rinse to spin, and now it doesn't shake.
Green Light! The spin is over, the longer job is done;
And what was washed is plastered to the walls from being spun.
You'd think the tub is empty, since the bottom's clear and bright;
I'm glad the spinning earth can't throw *us* out into the night!

For that is where we'd go, because the sky is not a wall;
But earth's content to hold us with our dirty shirts and all.
Still, spinning *is* a funny thing: the tub goes like a top.
The dryer, on the other hand, runs like a wheel. I plop
The damp unsorted pillowcases, hanks, and socks, and what
Into a kind of squirrel cage that generates a lot
Of heat when set at *Medium*. But this one needs the dime
I haven't got! I'll dry some other clothes some other time.

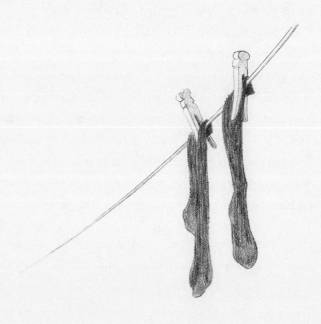

Human Beings

Some have a dog,
Some keep a bee,
Some own a horse;
But all of course
Must slap mosquitoes,
Same as we.

Some love to garden,
Plant a tree;
Some find the birds;
In other words,
They seed a feeder.
So do we.

Some like canaries;
Some agree
On goldfish, say.
Most stay away
From poison ivy.
So do we.

Some travel far,
Climb mountains, ski,
Or fly a plane.
But then, again,
Some watch TV;
And so do we.

Some praise the prairies,
Some the sea;
Some want it hot,
Some cool; but what
All get are colds.
And so do we.

Some dwell in cities,
Others flee
To suburbs way
Out; still, they pay
Their rent or taxes.
So do we.

First and Last

A tadpole hasn't a pole at all,
And he *doesn't* live in a hole in the wall.

You've got it wrong: a polecat's not
A cat on a pole. And I'll tell you what:

A bullfrog's never a bull; and how
Could a cowbird possibly be a cow?

A kingbird, though, *is* a kind of king,
And he chases a crow like anything.

Snowflakes

Sometime this winter if you go
To walk in soft new-falling snow
When flakes are big and come down slow

To settle on your sleeve as bright
As stars that couldn't wait for night,
You won't know what you have in sight —

Another world — unless you bring
A magnifying glass. This thing
We call a snowflake is the king

Of crystals. Do you like surprise?
Examine him three times his size:
At first you won't believe your eyes.

Stars look alike, but flakes do not:
No two the same in all the lot
That you will get in any spot

You chance to be, for every one
Come spinning through the sky has none
But his own window-wings of sun:

Joints, points, and crosses. What could make
Such lacework with no crack or break?
In billion billions, no mistake?

Answering Your Question

In grapes I know there *may* be seeds;
In prunes I know there will be.
My name is Shadwell Presswood Leeds,
My sister's name is Trilby.

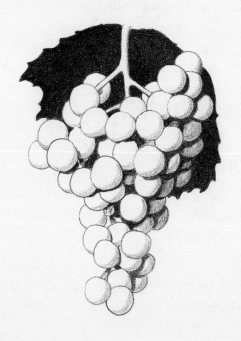

The Doctor

When the doctor comes
he always hums
Ta-dee, ta-diddle-doo;
which means a lot —
"Well, what have you got?"
"Hello!" or "How are *you?*"

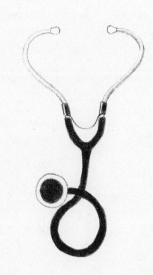

His bag is black,
I'm on my back.
Ta-dee, ta-diddle-o:
His stethoscope
will get the dope
on how things are below.

He hums his "Young
man, how's that tongue?"
Ta-dee, ta-diddle-dee:
I stick it out.
His hum's about
like language now to me.

With a snappy shake
(don't thermometers break?)
Ta-dee, ta-diddle-die:
he sticks it in
as I try to grin;
but he hums "Be quiet!" My,

what a hum-drum hum
if results are bum,
what tiddles and tas if slick.
Humming under his breath,
is he scared to death
of mumps? The hum goes quick

to a fast pulse. Oh,
but it idles slow
while fingers probe the jaw
for glands just not
I forget just what.
The throat? "Say ah-h-h, not *aw-w-w!*"

breaks *dee-diddle-doo*
right smack in two;

and he generally adds "Now, rest!"
when he goes. When he's gone,
though, his hum hangs on
in the stuff in the medicine chest.

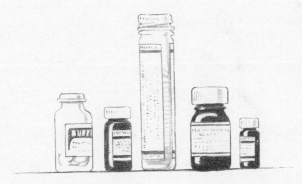

Hammock

Our hammock swings between two trees,
So when the garden's full of bees,
And if the hammock's full of me,
They fly right over, bee by bee.
They fly goshawful fast and straight —
I guess a bee is never late;
And if I can't quite see the line,
I try to think I hear the whine:
Much higher than the drowsy sound
Of having hives of bees around.
Provided bees don't bother me,
I'm glad to let a bee just be.
Some day I'll put a microphone
Inside their door and pipe the drone

Above my hammock, fall asleep
To bees all busy-buzz that keep
Their distance. Meanwhile here I lie.
I'm watching now a butterfly,
Unhurried, knowing not what's up:
A daisy, rose, or buttercup?
Not caring where he's been, or where
He's flapping to. He fills the air
With little flags and floats away
As I do on this summer's day.

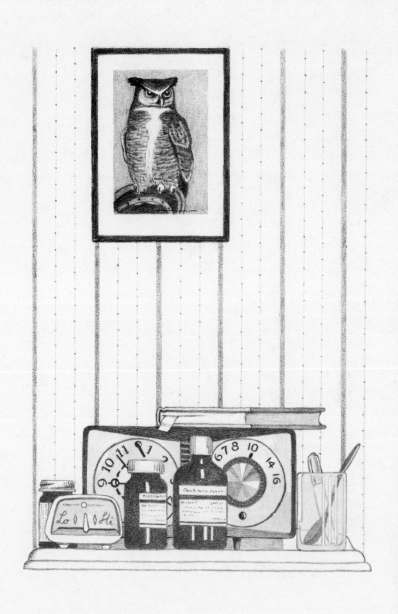

Breakfast

Morning? Morning will produce
a little orange of the juice;
and sure as surely I was born,
a little flaking of the corn,
a little glassing of the white
invention of the cow. Tonight,
though I might ask, might even beg,
to be a-scrambling for the egg,
for bacon sizzly on the fry —
that's not for me, me being I.
Me being I and what I am:
no bit of toast upon the jam,
no chance at creaming of the wheat,
or oating of the meal, to eat.

I meant to say that I'm in bed
and have the bug, the doctor said.

Fast and Slow

The Snail is slow. The swift Gazelle
Could never manage with a shell.

The Snail, without his shell, would squirm
And look a lot like half a worm.

To find him, you would need to peek
Inside some nasty robin's beak.

The poor Gazelle must run to stay
Alive. And that's about the way

It is with Snails and swift Gazelles:
Some have, and some do not have, shells.

Shrew

The little shrew is soricine.
He looks, though he is not, divine:
no animal so slick and sleek
can qualify as mild and meek.
A fighter, he can lick his weight
in anything except his mate.
He'll stand erect on his hind legs;
and if you think perhaps he begs,
he does — he begs you, man to shrew,
to meet him. Foolish if you do!
As you back off, then, far beneath
he lets you see his set of teeth.
Please don't mistake him for a mouse:
you wouldn't want him in your house.
So far as that goes, I'm aware
you may not want a mouse in there.

Secret

Jean said, *No.*
But Ruth said, *Yes!*
What? said Judy.
Gwyn said, *Guess!*
Where? said Karen.
There! said Claire.
But Lori's eyes said,
I don't care.

Mr. Bidery's Spidery Garden

Poor old Mr. Bidery.
His garden's awfully spidery:
Bugs use it as a hidery.

In April it was seedery,
By May a mess of weedery;
And oh, the bugs! How greedery.

White flowers out or buddery,
Potatoes made it spuddery;
And when it rained, what muddery!

June days grow long and shaddery;
Bullfrog forgets his taddery;
The spider legs his laddery.

With cabbages so odory,
Snapdragon soon explodery,
At twilight all is toadary.

Young corn still far from foddery,
No sign of goldenrodery,
Yet feeling low and doddery

Is poor old Mr. Bidery,
His garden lush and spidery,
His apples green, not cidery.

Pea-picking *is* so poddery!

Shiver My Timbers

Polly Vole
kept warm on coal;
Franklin Flinders,
ditto. Cinders
glowed like embers,
he remembers.
Humphry Hood
says gas was good;
and so were logs,
adds Billy Boggs.
Jerry Jove
preferred a stove.

Who now has any
such? Not many!
Some, inspired,
with houses wired
for volts and amps,
turn on their lamps.

You can't recycle
heat, says Michael
Pusey. Who's he
kidding? None
of us could squeak
by one more week
without the sun —
all said and done,
still Number One.

Melvin Martin Riley Smith

Melvin Martin Riley Smith
Made do without what we do with.
For instance, did he have a kite?
He didn't, but he had the right
Amount of string to make one fly,
And lots and lots and lots of sky.

Frog Music

In a boggy old bog
by a loggy old log
sat a froggy old frog.

He had spots on his skin;
on his face was a grin
that was wide and was thin.

He was green. He was fat
as an old Cheshire cat.
He was flat where he sat.

While he hoped that a fly
would fly by by-and-by,

it was also his wish
to avoid Mr. Fish,

Mr. Turtle, and tall
Mr. Heron, since all
of them *might* pay a call,

and just *might* be aware
of his grin, skin, and bare

bulgy head and those eyes,
very goggly in size.

So he grinned and just sat,
sat and sat, sat and sat,
looking silly like that.

But no fish saw him grin,
thinking, *Now* he'll jump in!

and no turtle a-cruise
thought him there in the ooze,

as a heron on one
leggy leg would have done.
Not a twitch in him — none.

Isn't life pretty grim
for a frog? Think of him.

But then think of that fly
flying by by-and-by.

LMNTL

"Albert, have you a turtle?"
I'll say to him, and Bert'll
say "Yes! Of *course* I have a turtle."

But if I write,
"Have you a trtl, Albert?"
(as I might)
I wonder if Brtl guess
just what I mean?

We all have seen
a dog's tail wagl,
haven't we?
We all agree
that what a dogldo,
a polywogl too.

We've hrd a brd, grls gigl;
observed how skwrls hnt
for nuts; how big pigs grnt;
know how we feel
on hearing young pigsqweel.

Bbbbs buzz, and ktns play;
bats flitrfly azootowls cry.

Why don't we *spell* that way?
Make ibx look like gnu?
Lfnts too; zbras inizoo?
I do. Do you?

Rain Song

The rain is driving silver nails
into the shingles overhead.
A little girl is playing scales;
she plays them as if something ails
her. Otherwise it's as I said:
The rain is driving silver nails
into the shingles overhead.

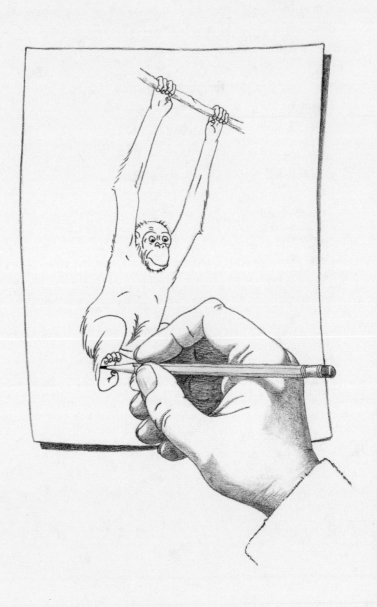

How to Draw a Monkey

To draw a monkey, don't begin
With him, but what he's on or in.
He's in a tree, he's on a limb,
Or was on one. Just follow him
Or follow me — it's all the same,
But easier with me: I'm tame.
You see the branch he's hanging from?
Don't draw it all, though. Just draw some
Of it — about two inches, say.
And draw it so it doesn't sway.
Next twist ten monkey fingers round
It, way up there above the ground,
And hang two arms from them, straight down.
(If you use color, make it brown.
And if the monkey has to scratch,
You'll have to change my method, natch!)
Now join those arms to shoulders, wide
Apart to keep the head inside.
If you can't make a monkey's face,
Look in the mirror! Then you place
The body underneath the head,
But full of life — he isn't dead;

He's just a monkey hanging there
Without his legs. But oh, beware
Of leaving him, forgetting legs!
Remember, chickens come from eggs,
But monkeys, unlike eggs, don't run:
Without two legs it isn't done.
Be sure that to each leg you add
One foot. And if your drawing pad
Is not quite long enough for toes,
Who cares? The monkey, I suppose.

Circus

Caleb likes a good sad clown,
Whose smile is always upside down.
He laughs straight through each foolish show,
With two clowns clowning it below:
One has a gun that he can toot,
One has a horn that he can shoot!
Then Caleb sits and licks the spun
White sugar. Said sad clowns are fun.

Luke (three) prefers the flying rings,
And jugglers who can manage things
And keep them festive in the air.
He also flips before the bear
Who walks flat-foot and shaggy, likes
To balance balls and pedal bikes.
Around his nose he has a strap
(The bear does). Luke has mother's lap.

Theresa, born to ride, is awed
By this big black whose back is broad;
Whose whipless queen in golden gown
Can waltz, cavort, or kneel him down,
Then gallop round in one mad swirl
Of skirt, a frantic act. "The girl —
The queen — leaned back, blew kisses. Gee!
She blew one my way, too," says T.

Wizzle

I saw that wizzlebug a-wozzle,
drinking from the plastic nozzle
of the plastic hose a-drizzle
by the peonies. Well, his'll
be a harder time tomorrow
when he comes to drown his sorrow!
I'll turn the wizzle — I mean faucet —
off, if I can come across it.
All these wizzlebugs are cheeky;
lucky when the water's leaky.
Gulpy-glop, you've heard them drinking?
Sounds just like a sink that's sinking.

Marty's Party

Marty's party?
Jamie came. He
seemed to Judy
dreadful rude. He
joggled Davy,
spilled his gravy,
squeezed a melon
seed at Helen,
gave a poke so
Eddy's Coke so
fresh and fizzy
showered Lizzy;
jostled Frank
who dropped a hank
of juicy candy.
Debby handy —
double bubble
gum in trouble —

Debbie mebbie
stumbled, bumbled
into Jessie.
Very messy!
Very sticky!

That's a quickie —
not so ludi-
crous to Judy,
watching Jamie
jilting Amy,
wilting Mamie,
finding Vicky.

What a tricky
lad! Where's Marty?
Don't know. She just
gave the party.

Louinda

Louinda is a pretty name:
I've never seen or heard it, though.
I think that you can say the same:
Louinda *is* a pretty name.
Please tell Louella what I owe
To Linda. As I say below,
Louinda is a pretty name.
I've never seen or heard it, though.

Little

Little wind, little sun,
Little tree — only one.
Little bird, little wing,
Little song he can sing.
Little need he should stay,
Little *up*-now, away
Little speck, and he's far
Where all little things are.
Little things for me too:
Little sad that he flew.

Sometimes

The clouds are full of new blue sky,
The water's full of sea;
The apples full of deep-dish pie,
And I am full of me.

My money's full of pockets too,
My teeth are full of jaw;
The animals are full of zoo,
The cole is full of slaw.

How full things are of this or that:
The tea so full of spoon;
The wurst so very full of brat,
The shine brimful of moon.

Whistle

I'm talking of a little train whose mother is a Diesel,
And how it skins around a curve as slippery as a
      weasel;
While now and then young Whistle clears his throat
      to give a toot —
You ought to hear him! Mother Diesel thinks he's
      very cute.

One day this little train was flying fast, but on the
      straight:
It carried twenty passengers and lots and lots of
      freight;
And coming to one crossing — reddish lights (left-
      right) a-blink —
Young Whistle, as was usual, thought "I ought to
      blow, I think."

The engineer thought likewise, but what issued was a
      fiz-z-z-z-z.
"There's something wrong with Whistle," said his
      mother. "See what is!"
She said it to the engineer, whose hand was on the
      throttle;
His pipe was in his mouth and full of — well, *you*
      know — of dottle.

He said he hadn't time to look at Whistle: "We're
　　behind."
He didn't say behind just what, of course, but never
　　mind.
He didn't mind; but Whistle did, and whispered to
　　his mother.
(You try to whisper fizzy-fizz: one fizz sounds like
　　another.)

His mother gulped a gulp of oil, and in a little gauge
(The engineer had filled his pipe) she let him see
　　her rage.
"Now, Mother, take it easy! Don't you think it's just
　　a frog
In Whistle's throat? It isn't night; there isn't any fog.

"The sun is bright and chipper. I can see a mile
　　ahead."
"Would Whistle whisper to me if there's nothing to
　　be said?"
The pipe was lit and drawing well, the window open
　　wide;
So engineer reflected: *Was* there something down
　　inside

Of Whistle's throat? A gnat? An ant? A June bug
　　in July?
If Whistle couldn't whistle . . . "Well, it's nice to
　　have him try,"

The engineer was saying — took his pipe out so he
    could.
He'd run a cleaner through it. The tobacco tasted
    good.

There wasn't any cleaner, though, to ram down
    Whistle's throat.
He couldn't use a gargle for the gurgle of one note.
What *was* his note? The engineer confessed he didn't
    know.
His Diesel mother thought it was B flat — the B below

The really truly B, the one above the middle C.
(Just look at your piano — C D E F G A B.)
"What difference does it make?" The engineer blew
    bluish smoke.
"I wish" — Ma Diesel rumbled as she said it — "you
    would poke

"Your finger into Whistle. Slow me up or slow me
    down;
You've got to do it anyway, we're coming to a town."
The engineer said, "Mother, gosh! You're living in
    a dream!
Your grampa had a whistle, but he blew himself by
    steam.

"We make a lot of steam on board, but you know
      where it goes:
We heat the coaches with it — ten times everybody's
      toes
Depend on it in winter. We don't make it now.
      Today
It wouldn't work for Whistle — he's electric all the
      way,

"With diaphragm and wires and stuff, just like a
      telephone;
And only sound comes out of him — not steam —
      when he is blown.
That's how it is. Don't *you* forget what makes *you*
      run! It's oil.
We haven't got the steam to bring a bantam's egg
      to boil.

"I tell you what we'll do: at milepost 60 we'll be on
The siding, and the Hanker Chief will thunder by,
      be gone,
Before you say 'Jack Robinson' — who, by the way,
      was Jack?
But just before he does it, coming down the single
      track,

"He'll blow his nose — a friendly blast of greeting.
You've got ears,
And obviously you'll hear it. Whistle will. So calm
your fears.
I'll pull the cord and close the circuit, ready for the
note
That Hanker Chief will thistle into our young
Whistle's throat.

"I'll bet you all the air that's in your brakes — I
hope you've *some* —
Young Whistle will respond the way drums vibrate,
drum to drum."
And sure enough, when Hanker Chief shot by in
clouds of dust,
Old Mother Diesel heard the blast — the engineer
had thrust

*His fingers in his ears — and Whistle blew as fit to
bust!*

Then Mother rolled them back again upon the
welded rails.
Young Whistle gave a toot, and since that day he
never fails
To blow when he is needed. Mother Diesel has no
gripe.
The engineer has trouble, though, with dottle in his
pipe.

Trinity Place

(A Christmas Card for Louis M. Lyons)

With light enough on clean fresh-fallen snow,
Tracks managed with good-by to say hello.
I looked at three before I let them go.

One was a child's: a boy or girl whose name
Was nothing. But two footprints not the same —
One clear, one fainter — meant the child was lame.

The second tracks were dog and plainly said
I'm lost. The leash by which he had been led
Was dragging like one runner on a sled.

The other tracks were bird on windowsill
Where one had fluffed his feathers and sat still,
Not for the bread but sunglare in the chill.

The child would pass, I knew, the little shop
With windows full of toys. The tracks would stop.
The dog perhaps would find the friendly cop.

And last the hungry bird, when night should come,
Would search the wider sill without a crumb.
But such is Christmas in the snow for some.

Runover Rhyme

Down by the pool still fishing,
Wishing for fish, I fail;
Praying for birds not present,
Pheasant or grouse or quail.

Up in the woods, his hammer
Stammering, I can't see
The woodpecker, find the cunning
Sunning old owl in tree.

Over the field such raucous
Talk as the crows talk on!
Nothing around me slumbers;
Numbers of birds have gone.

Even the leaves hang listless,
Lasting through days we lose,
Empty of what is wanted,
Haunted by what we choose.

The Wave

As I went up October Street,
a windblown wave of leaves to greet
me broke away from someone's lawn.
I thought of sands that I'd been on,
where waves like this came dancing in
to spread their foam out very thin.
These leaves, though, hadn't any foam
or beach on which to roll in home;
they just put up one ragged line
of tumble-turn and intertwine,
all yellow-gold and bronzy-red;
and when the breeze had died or fled,
the wave lay like a jumping rope
with which the children couldn't cope —
all curves and kinks, with none to take
the ends and give it one good shake.

The Likes and Looks of Letters

Like roundish letters — *o c u?*
You do or don't? Can't say? OK.
I like them tall: *b d h l,*
much better, in a way. I'll spell
some tall ones doubled: paddle, drill,
bib, bobble, bulb, withhold;
or quill, dwell, sellout, silly, deed —
all simple words for us to read;
all talls: heighho, wild, wold;
To which I add a word for *z:*
snooze, sneeze, jazz, sizzle, drizzle, breeze,
buzz, nuzzle, nozzle, frazzle, freeze,
do something odd to me!

I've got to go now. *You* take up
dropped letters; those that go
straight down — *j p:* pip, pup,
jeep, jujube. *J*'s don't double, though;
but *p*'s are doubling all the time
in ripple, apple, topple, stipple. . . .
Tired of this rhyme?
$\qquad\qquad$ I'm.

Harvestman

Old Daddy Longlegs, Harvestman,
travels with no particular plan
in mind, so far as I can see:
I meet him wherever he happens to be.
In summer he happens most of all
to be on the sunniest pineboard wall
of a house by a lake. So I say "Hello!
That's a splintery board for stubbing a toe."
He doesn't have toes, of course, but what
do you say to a creature that looks a lot
like a tiny bright pebble with hand-me-down legs,
not a bit good for much except walking on eggs?

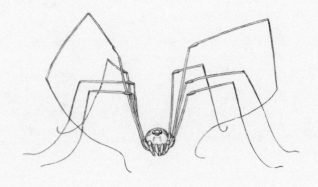

In Winter Sky

Late afternoon: clouds made a hole.
Sun put two fingers through and stole
The golden tops of three or four
Big trees. He would have stolen more;
But clouds, not liking what he did,
Closed up the hole and clapped a lid
On all the trees that they could sight.
Sun whipped his swords out for a fight,
Slashed into them. Each blade he thrust
Shone like a stairwell full of dust
With crosslight on it. Lots of trees
Held up their fiery shields to these.
The clouds, now cut to ribbons, red
With evening blood, closed ranks and fled.

Suddenly

All over the fields there was ice today,
and everybody was out on skates.
It had rained through Christmas, raining away
on the snow, but then in the night the Fates,
or whatever it is that decides to freeze,
had dropped the temperature twenty degrees,
and here were the fields like dinner plates
in the shine and flash of the morning sun;
and never, I think, had the kids such fun
as they had on a Christmas day plus one!

Wide fields, big fields, with not any trees:
Skate where you would, and do as you please.
It wasn't just hockey and blow your nose
and lose your mittens and freeze your toes:
It was out and beyond and away on the crust
that was ice you could bend over land you could
                    trust.
It was something so wonderful, barely begun,
yet on into moonlight, to over-and-done;
it was skating where no one had skated before,
through field after field till there weren't any more.

It was something just given you — yours by right;
though perhaps you didn't deserve it, quite.

Big Question

Why do you lose things this way?
Why do you say:
I don't choosa lose 'em,
eh?
You lose 'em,
hide 'em
ad infinidem;
whether you read 'em, need 'em,
ride 'em,
or have scarcely tried 'em;
play 'em or break 'em,
people don't make 'em
but you just take 'em,
wind 'em, bounce 'em, renounce 'em,
beat 'em, trounce 'em,
and then can't find 'em!

Bells lose their peals;
You'd lose your meals
And I'd have to repeat 'em
If you didn't eat 'em!

'em'em'em'em'em'em'em'em'em'em'em'em'em'em'em'em

When I Would Travel

When I would travel, I take down
a book like one of yours —
blue binding, is it? yellow? brown? —
itself a book of tours

for which I neither leave the page
nor pause to pack a bag.
I know the language, place, and age:
the country of no flag,

where I am welcome, as are you.
Clouds freckle up the west;
the sun is rising on the view.
Where is it? Who has guessed?

But let me travel far as far
is far, that nameless book,
or one much like it — like a star,
a mountaintop, a brook —

is there beside me, so that I
may journey secretly
beyond myself, as by and by
for you it so may be.

Summer Shower

Window window window pane:
Let it let it let it rain
Drop by drop by drop by drop.

Run your rivers from the top
Zigzaggy down, like slow wet forks
Of lightning, so the slippery corks
Of bubbles float and overtake
Each other till three bubbles make
A kind of boat too fat to fit
The river. That's the end of it.
>   Straight
>   down
>   it
>   slides
>   and
>   with
>   a
>   splash
Is lost against the window sash.

Window window window pane:
Let it let it let it rain.

No Present Like the Time

"No time like the present," they always used to say,
Meaning — *Busy! Do You Hear Me? Don't Delay!*
Much better in reverse (it doesn't have to rhyme):
Simply, simply, *No present like the time.*

Time, you agree, is everybody's gift,
But the packages aren't the same.
The lid of each is there to lift,
Yet only one package bears your name.

Lift the lid a little now each morning,
And what comes whistling out?
A day's supply of time. Almost a-borning
It dies with every breath as you go about

Your work or play. How much of it is in
That package? No one knows. You, least of all.
Time is indifferent to what we begin;
Indifferent also to whether we stand or fall.

"Don't waste your time," they say. Waste time you will;
And such as you wish, of course, is yours to squander.
Don't call it wasted when you climb a hill!
Through fields and woods to wander

Is to be young, and time belongs to the young.
It's when you're old that clocks begin to tick.
Play fair with time: his praise so rarely sung.
He is your snail. But oh, his pulse is quick.

The Trouble Was Simply That

the boy wasn't ready for a hat.
The hat, though, was ready for him:
nice crown, good lining, broad brim.
So many people go hatless!
Put your finger down on an atlas —
on land, of course, not on the sea —
and the chances are two to three
the people there go bareheaded.
Some needles just *won't* be threaded;
some heads just refuse to be hatted;
some dogs don't like to be patted;
some shirts don't want to be buttoned;
most sheep dislike to be muttoned.
Few cucumbers crave to be pickled;
fat tummies (ha, ha) are not tickled.

The trouble is just as I said:
Seen a boy with no hat on his head?

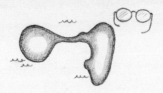

Islands in Boston Harbor

How many islands in the bay?
About a hundred, so they say.
I hope they'll all be there today!

Few people know them. Few can boast
They've been on one and seen the ghost
Of Captain Kidd perhaps — almost.

Down on the map they look so queer:
Unvisited, remote, and drear,
They might be miles away from here.

Down on the map you can't see where
The pirates hid, when they were there.
One island looks just like a pair

Of spectacles; one's like a whale,
And one's a fish without a tail,
And one's a ship without a sail.

Still others seem what they are not:
Napoleon's boot, the moon, and what
Might be a fat smoked ham. A lot

Is in one's island point of view:
The boat I'm on will pass a few.
You look at them. They look at you.

The best have beaches, trees, and rocks,
And cormorants, and gulls in flocks;
But some are faced with granite blocks

Where ancient forts for guns and stuff
Were used by us when times were tough.
Of islands, who can have enough?

Some day a boat will land me right
Upon the shore of one — it might.
And would *I* be a welcome sight!

Just all that island: none but me,
Exploring everything — free, free!
And everywhere — the sea, the sea!

Who Hasn't Played Gazintas?

In your arithmetics
the *problem* is what sticks.
The language isn't bound
by spelling, but by sound.
So 3 gazinta 81.
The answer? 27. Done!
In *long* division, I would hint, a
lot of work gazin gazinta.

Or maybe you like Adams — what?
To add 'em up is Adams' lot.
So when you look for something more,
let Adams help you with it. 4
plus half of nine-nine-nine — *precise!*

Well, minusing is also nice.
Take 45, and take it twice
from 93. That's three for me;
And even Mr. Minus, he
can't come much closer, you'll agree.

Then Tums: the sign of which is *x*.
Do 8 tums 1-5-6? It checks
at just one thousand two four eight.
Repeat: 1,248.

Computers work at a faster rate.

Exit x

Let x be this
and y be that,
my teacher says. And I
expecting x to be complex
enough, put wily y
to work. If *vex*
is x^2, *rex*
will equal one-no-three.
But that's not why
x over my
right shoulder laughs at me.

Look: What Am I?

Old friend of man, and made
to slice through root and blade
of grass or weed. The earth was laid
for me to turn.
Up, then down I go,
as sure as I am slow.
What am I?
Spade.

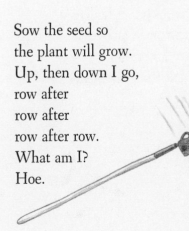

Sow the seed so
the plant will grow.
Up, then down I go,
row after
row after
row after row.
What am I?
Hoe.

In frontier days lean lads
built cabins; dads, granddads
hewed all the beams. Young tads
watched how the strong backs bent.
Up, then down I went.
What am I?
Adze . . . *What?*
Adze.

Out at the woodlot's edge
if you would have the wedge
split clean as privet hedge,
go eat your meat and veg.
Up, then down I go.
To strike it true, my pledge!
What am I?
Sledge.

He who good firewood stacks
knows that my bright head packs
a wallop the hatchet lacks.
Up, then down I go:
I am as nails to tacks.
Watch out below!
What am I?
Ax.

Across the board you draw
one line. The pine smells raw.
Up, then down I go,
just like a jaw
with a juicy chaw
in it. And do I spit!
What am I?
Saw.

Nails are my game: I stammer,
saying things over. Glamour
I never knew.
Up, then down I go.
Who gets me on his thumb
not silent is, but dumb!
What am I?
Hammer.

Eating at the Restaurant of How Chow Now

Ever eaten Chinese food?
Eaten with chopsticks made of wood,
Holding one chopstick nice and tight?
The other never works just right.

Or if it does, the tight one teeters.
These wooden hinges aren't for eaters
Like you and me. We get a grip
On bamboo shoots, and off they slip!

Thin mushroom slices, peapods, rice,
Hockeypuck meat, need some device
to gather in and underslide them.
Forks are good. But Chinese hide them.

Same with knives: *they can't abide them!*

Under the White Pine

Where the fine pine
by the lone stone

spreads a red bed
for the blown cone,

all the blade shade
fills the green scene.

Keep your cool pool!
Let me lean clean,

with a slack back
to the tall wall

of my own stone,
hear the fall call

of the stray jay
drown the *dee-dee*

chickas say say;
know the slow crow

far away, gley
when his *caw caw*

means but *hey! hey!*
Watch a squirrel curl

round a slim limb;
see him creep, leap

through the dim gym
tops of trees . . . Bees,

up the day's haze,
wing in light flight

with a drone tone,
needing night sight

in the live hive.   .   .
So it blends, ends

as on dark bark
fails the sun:
                    one

longs to praise days,
heave a high sigh

through the boughs!
                    How's
one to try . . . try?

Queer Story of the Fowse or Fox

(*owse, owsen* is the Scottish variation of *ox, oxen*)

Beyond a whopping owse or ox,
behind his fence a fowse or fox,
investigating rowse or rocks,
has pounced upon a mouse or mox
and flushed a lady grouse or grox,
reminding him of flowse or flocks
of chickens of intowse-intox-
icating scents. The house- or hox-
dog barks just then. That louse or lox
is half and half — half dowse, half dox.
In Reynard's mind, a powse or pox
on *him!* He turns and cowse or cocks
his head. My presence shouse or shocks
him. Exit, then, that fowse or fox,
which leaves me with the owse or ox.

Plymouth Rocks, of Course

I've got three hens. A rooster? No.
He'd dislike laying eggs, and so
I've got three hens. Sometimes they lay;
at first they laid three eggs a day.
It's usually one now; never none.
I don't think hens think eggs are fun.
I feed them corn, wheat, oats, and bran,
and mix hot bran mash in a pan.
I give them grit and oyster shells
and other things the feedstore sells,
including some queer stinko stuff
to make them lay more eggs. It's tough
to be a hen and have to eat
that gravelly grit. And it's no treat
to swallow oyster shells cut fine.
The thought still shivers down my spine!
But hens have crops where shells and grit
grind corn and wheat and oats. And it
seems dandy just to have no teeth
and do your chewing underneath
your throat — all automatic, too;
no mouth to wipe when you are through.
The dirty job, of course, is when
I clean the chicken house. A hen
needs lots of exercise: she'll scratch
the straw back little patch by patch

to find the stuff I've scattered. She
may sing a little song to me
that's nothing like her cackle noise,
but soft and sweet. For who enjoys
life more than happy hens? The cows,
perhaps. They have no crops, but browse
a while and then rechew the hay
as cud which they had tucked away
in stomach number one for storage.
Forget the cows, and let them forage.
I meant to talk about just how
my hens are doing up to now.

More or Less

Add one letter to *widow*,
and that's what you can see through;
but add it after that to *doe*,
by doing so you'll *be* through.
One letter more in *solder*
means lead, not solder, he'll shoot;
and another one added to His *Hon.*
makes something His Hon. can toot.

Now take one letter from *tables*,
and you are ready to tell them;
subtract a different one from *grasses*,
and you can easily smell them.
One letter out of *shout* might mean
that something could well be dead.
If another is dropped from *hate* — well, you
can put what is left on your head!

Strike out what letters from *fancy*
to make yourself feel cooler?
Or what (a lot) from *pinching*
for something found on a ruler?
Delete a little from *tower*,
the result is yours to wiggle;
and, lastly, a smidgen more from *engage*
for some words to make you giggle.

The Look and Sound of Words

You *know* the word *cathedral*.
How about *tetartohedral*?
There's a grass that's called *esparto*,
Which is pretty; but tet-tar-toe,
Plus the *heed-ral* sound just after,
Seems as musical as laughter.

Words *look* at you. In saying
"Look at *me!*" they see you weighing
All their syllables — the "l's" and
"esses" specially — the bells and
Brightness of their being. So you
Say, "Gee whiz! I *know* you!"

Words have more to them than meaning:
Words like *equidistant, gleaning,*
Paradoxical, and *glisten.*
All you have to do is *listen.*
That's the way words come to settle
In your mind like molten metal.

When they cool, you won't believe you
Aren't old friends. They'll *never* leave you.

440

The Game of Doublets

This is a game that Lewis Carroll played,
Called "Doublets." He invented it and made
These rules: Select *two* short words — opposite
In sense, like SNOW and RAIN, or OUT and LIT —
Or else two words which, saying them, we link:
DUCK SOUP; COMB HAIR; perhaps PLAY
      BALL: FURS MINK;
Or two *five*-letter words like BREAD and TOAST.

Now in these few examples *What is most
Important*? Why, that any pairs you choose
Have each *three* letters, *four*, or *five*. Don't use
Six-letter words, or longer, for the trick
Is how to get the *first* word changed as quick —
Excuse me, *quickly* — as you ever can
Into the other: APE (say) into MAN.
How do you change it? Well, you make a chain
Of words that run like this — so have them plain
And full in capitals — LIT BIT BUT OUT.

You see at once just what to do, no doubt.
Remove *one* letter from the *first* word, then
Replace it with another: LIT BIT. When
You do this, put the new one *right smack back*
From where you took the first one. LIT will lack

The L, and so the B goes there and makes
A new word (BIT). You will have made mistakes
If you should jump for WIT or FIT or PIT.
With BIT, though, as the I comes out of it,
In goes the U for BUT; and you see what
The next step is: *remove the B*. You've got
Your O all ready? In? Indeed! OUT! *There!*
I made that up for you, and I can spare
Another: FISH *WISH* WISE WINE LINE. It's
          wrong
To think they're all that easy, though, for long
Ago (just ninety years) the man who wrote
You *Alice* (which you've read) took off his coat

And went to work on Doublets: APE to MAN!
So simple! APE *ARE ERE ERR EAR MAR* MAN.
There's poetry in that — the sound of it:
Ape *are* ere *err* ear *mar* man — *words* that *flit*
Across the page! That is a harder one
Than those we started with, but lots more fun.

This is the place, I guess, where I explain
The *fewer* links you have in every chain,
The better. So, if two of you compete,
The *shorter* chain will win. APE-MAN's complete
With *five* links in the chain (that's ARE through
          MAR).
Take Mr. Carroll's WET DRY. Here you are:

WET *BET BEY DEY* DRY — *three* links; two are
      tough:
BEY, DEY are generals.* But that's enough
Of quick short doublets. No? Well, this EYE LID
Is Carroll's: EYE *DYE DIE DID* LID. I bid
You try a new one (mine). Quite hard: SNOW RAIN.
I started wrong: SNOW *STOW STEW STEM* . . .
      In vain
I tried to run it into RAIN from there.

Try it yourself! You'll likely get nowhere.
Then I went back and used a different ploy:
SNOW *SLOW SLEW SLED SLID* SAID . . .
      and then, O boy!
I saw the finish . . . RAID to RAIN. How fares
The game? You might make up some brand-new pairs
Of words. Or take, from Mr. Carroll's bunch,
PIG (*WIG WAG WAY* SAY) STY; or after lunch
WHEAT BREAD, TREE WOOD, GRASS
      GREEN, TEA HOT, MINE COAL,
ONE TWO, PINK BLUE, ELM OAK, GRUB
      MOTH, RICE BOWL.
Or set your sights at changing CAIN to ABEL.
(One hint: begin with CHIN.) Or ask Aunt Mabel
If she would like a meaty one with gravy
On *seven* links of sausage: ARMY NAVY.

* Look them up in the dictionary.

443

NOTE: PLAY BALL seems to require *nine* links: PLAY pray pram prim grim grin gain pain pail pall BALL. Perhaps you can solve it with fewer. Let me now suggest, as an extension of Mr. Carroll's idea, a Triplet Game, in which one would choose three words, each having some relation to the other pair. Take SKY SUN DAY, which almost solves itself: SKY say pay pan pun SUN pun pan pay DAY. Here is another which looks hard and probably is: COME OVER HERE. *You* try it. I need a rest. Oh, I forgot: CAIN to ABEL: CAIN chin shin shun spun spud sped aped abed ABEL.

L.CARROLL-Gamester

Inside Information

("I," sitting down with "J,"
said: Well, what shall we play?)

Debbie is in DEBt.
You see her? DEB — *B* plus a *t?*
And Sue is there in SUEt,
isn't she? OK. But gee
whiz! Sal's in SALt, as Dot's in DOTe,
as Tim's in TIMe.
I'd have you note
there's nothing to it:
Tom's in TOMe. . . .
so goes our rime,
so goes our pome.

Take Sam in SAMe,
or Tam in TAMe.
See Vi in VIm?
See Di in DIm?
See Mo in MOb?
See Jo in JOb?
Where's Gus? In GUSt;
Yes, Wes in WESt;
Rus turns to RUSt,
Jes speaks in JESt;

Pat pats his PATe;
Fat's fat. That's FATe.

"I," resting now, and ditto "J,"
exhausted from the game they play,
leave Stan in STANd just standing cold.
Poor Rob in ROBe, poor Sol in SOLd!
But if you're wise — what's called a savant —
you'll find some other names they haven't.

"I'm happy" — "I" says, "as a clam
Immersed in Coke." "J"'s in the Jam.

Ten Nights Before Christmas

"I don't believe in Santa Claus," says Number One.

"I do," says Number Two. "He weighs a ton."

"Couldn't come down *our* chimney, weighing that!"

"You haven't got a chimney one small bat
Could dive down through; but *he* could, though.
There's something magic about the places he can go."

"All that reindeer stuff and a sackful of toys,
And the bunch of North Pole gnomes that he em-
     ploys . . ."

"You hang up your stocking, don't you?" Number One
        says "Yes."
"I thought you did. Full enough in the A.M., I guess?"

"Sure. But that's an inside job. My Dad . . ."

"I know. You woke and saw him?"

                                    "Wish I had."

"So you *didn't* see him, eh? Of course not! Yet
You don't believe in a Santa Claus you haven't met."

"I can meet one in any downtown store . . ."

"They're for the birds and bipeds under four!
Look: last year I just *thought* of something I wanted
        a lot.
I didn't *tell* anyone. What do you think I got?
I won't tell *you;* but I *got* it. Now don't think too big."

"Could he get down our chimney with all that rig?"

"See? You don't know enough to say 'No Santa,' do
        you?
Does that do something to you?"

Pease Porridge Poems

1
Mustard when it's hot,
Custard when it's not.

2
Let tapioca share with *you*
These lidless fisheyes in the glue.

3
O summer squash! How posh!
All other squashes taste like galoshes.

4
What is parsley good for?
Gone for good!

It *couldn't* be! It *can't* be!
How I wish it could!

5
Eggplant has a lovely color.
As food, though, how could *anything* be duller?

6
Celery, if you braise it.
Raw celery? *You* praise it.

7

The nearest I come to a cow and her cud
Is when I relax with a fine baked spud.

8

Lens (a Latin word) is what a lentil *looks* like.
A soupy pot of Boston beans is what a lentil *cooks* like.

9

I love a pickle, but detest a cuke.
Please save your stamp and spare me the rebuke.

Just Around the Corner

Just around the corner!
Do you know
that just around the corner's where I go?
I always shiver when I feel
that just around the corner real
things happen, could be happening.
A dozen pigeons on the wing
went by just now. What made them fly?

You need a round-the-corner eye
to answer *that*. But something's up.
A boy is walking with his pup;
or, as I see it, pup has got
a boy upon a leash. They trot.
And round the corner, where he goes,
the puppy's round-the-corner nose
is pulling him. A whistle blew.
But that was round the corner too.
It's where some men in red tin hats
are building up a building that's
all boarded round; but there's a hole
that I can look through like a mole.
They're in a sort of cellar still.
A pump is pumping water till
it gushes from a pipe and flows
along the gutter. Down it goes

to fill the drain (that's just around
the corner) with a gurgly sound.
I hear a siren wailing now.
Some people turn and stare. But how
am I to tell which way the red
fire engine, hook and ladder, sped?
It's just around the corner where
you get to *see* things. Over there
across my street, Apartment Three
looks round the corner. That's not me,
my face glued to the window, though.
I'd be excited and I'd blow
right out the door!
I say once more:

Just around the corner shines the sun;
and just around the corner's where I run.

Make Merry

Make merry, child, make merry:
The day slips by so soon.
Make merry now, this very
Morning. Merry afternoon
will follow, and old Antiquary
Night will bury those unwary
Ere they ever made Make Merry.

Merry child, make merry!
The sound of laughter dies
So quickly, so contrary
Are the wayward cloudy skies.
Down adown adown down derry,
Cheeks as bright and red as cherry:
Merry, merry, make you merry!

456

Pamela

Pamela — you may call her that —
is making a witch's cloak and hat
for Halloween. She has a broom
up in the closet of her room.

Pamela says each night she tries
to dream of a youngish witch who flies.
The trouble with witches, according to Pam:
"They're all too old; and here I am

just seven. Somehow, I've got the itch.
Why shouldn't I learn to be a witch?
To fly out where it is they fly?
In pictures they are never high

above the ground; yet no one knows
where a witch has come from or where she goes!
I mean to start by the apple tree.
If a witch is there, be sure it's me.

It's mostly kids I'll scare — not you.
I don't know what my broom can do
by way of speed. If dreams work out
the way I think they will, no doubt

I'll get to Tiny Clark's all right.
At least I did the other night.
A practice dream, *that* was. I cleared
the garden wall, and then I steered

right over Tiny's rabbit hutch.
The rabbits didn't like it much.
I saw them — three wild streaks of white —
all every which way in their fright.

Then something woke me." Pam won't say
what woke her. She won't get away
with all this witch stuff, broom or not.
She dreams too much, and talks a lot.

of nonsense. Everyone knows *that*.
And with a witch's cloak and hat
and broom on Halloween, you'll see!
But I guess I'll watch that apple tree.

Birds in the Rain

The yellow warblers, the chickadee,
And four of the robins are in that tree,
Under the leaves until the storm
Gives the earth back to the sun to warm.

The rain came hard in a wanted burst,
And pools on the lawn will stop the thirst
Of all our birds. When? When the weather
Clears and they venture out together.

Even the trees are letting through
Some of the sky to where they flew,
Dripping the wings that bore them in,
And bird-breast sodden to the skin.

Between our house and the one deserted,
Lines of a silver blade inserted
Tell me the sun is driving back
The lightning and the cloud attack;

And soon the pleasure of the lawn
Shall be for birds to fare upon,
And the brave robin after worms
Since he has brought the rain to terms.

Hot Line to the Nursery

FATHER SPEAKING. What is that awful noise?

JANET. Hello?

FATHER. I said, *what* is that awful noise?

JANET. Stevie.

FATHER. Stevie, what is that awful noise?

STEVIE. Johnjo.

FATHER. *Johnjo?* Why, he can't . . .

STEVIE. Yes, he can too.

FATHER. Johnjo!

JOHNJO. Goo.

FATHER. Janet!

JANET. Father? OK. Over.

FATHER. Over my knee, young lady!

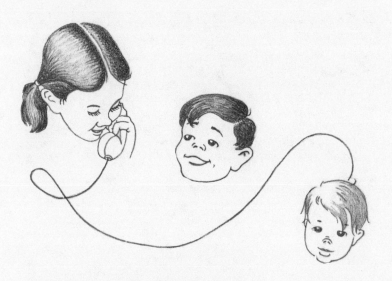

JANET. Father, Stevie knows something.

FATHER. What does Stevie know?

JANET. He won't tell me.

FATHER. Well, you tell him I want that *awful* noise
to *stop!*

JANET (*to Stevie*). He wants that *awful* noise to *stop!*

STEVIE. What awful noise?

JANET. Any awful noise, I guess.

FATHER (*listening*). No, not *any* noise. Just *that* noise!

JANET. OK. Do you want to speak to Johnjo again?

FATHER. No.

JANET. OK. Say OK, Johnjo.

JOHNJO. Goo!

Write Me Another Verse

In a book of mine called *Take Sky* (1962) I included some poems under the title "Write Me a Verse." (See pages 171–186.) These poems attempt to show the reader how to write a two-line verse, which is called a *couplet;* how to write a four-line verse, which is called a *quatrain;* how to write the five-line verse called the *limerick;* and how to write the eight-line verse called the *triolet.* All the directions in each case are given *in the verse-form itself.* That is, I talk in couplets, quatrains, limericks, and triolets.

In this section of the book which you have in your hand, you will find that I have carried this idea six steps farther. In "Write Me Another Verse" you will learn—or at least you *should* learn if you read carefully—how to write the *ballade* (which is *not* a ballad), the *tercet,* the *villanelle,* the *clerihew* (a verse-form invented by an Englishman named Edmund Clerihew Bentley), the *cinquain,* and *haiku.* You are probably familiar with haiku and the cinquain. The ballade may seem difficult, and it is. The villanelle is much less difficult, *but you should become familiar with the tercet before you attempt a villanelle.* The clerihew is tricky, but actually quite easy to write.

You will see that I have not bothered you here with talk about rhyme scheme, meter, and all that. Just read the first tercet, the first villanelle and the first ballade carefully and you can't go wrong! The *second* villanelle and the *second* ballade don't talk about technique; neither does the *second* tercet. When you come to the clerihew, cinquain, and haiku, just study *the first two or three examples,* and then you will be on your own. Be glad that you are. Plunge ahead!

One last word. Whenever you have written a poem of any sort, *always* read it aloud to yourself many times to make sure that your meter (rhythm) is correct, that your rhyme-words are the words you were looking for and *not* words forced upon you because you could not think of anything else. Above all: read the poem slowly and never in a singsong manner. Any poem, if it is any good at all, has life in it. You can kill it (I can kill it) by reading it in a dead-level voice.

The Tercet

(*pronounced* túr-set)

A tercet is a stanza of three lines,
All rhyming; like a pitchfork with three tines.
Or like three stars if none of them outshines

The others. Tercets have a natural grace,
And move along like this in easy pace,
And look up at you face to face to face.

But you can change the rhyme scheme as you wish.
When you go fishing and you bait your hook,
The thing you hope to catch, of course, is fish.

And so with writing tercets. Now I look
For some fresh other rhyme that I can squeeze
In there as with the *hook* and *look* I took

To brighten up this poem. Can a tercet breeze
Into the next this way? Well, so it seems.
Why not? If now we let this third line freeze,

We're back to where we started. On with *dreams!* —
An old poetic word at once redeems
Our one-rhyme scheme. I could go on for reams

Of paper, but I think by now you see
How pleasant tercets are to write. Write me,
Should you have trouble with them. Here I be.

Gone

I've looked behind the shed
And under every bed:
I think he must be dead.

What reason for alarm?
He doesn't know the farm.
I *knew* he'd come to harm!

He was a city one
Who never had begun
To think the city fun.

Now where could he have got?
He doesn't know a lot.
I haven't heard a shot.

That old abandoned well,
I thought. Perhaps he fell?
He didn't. I could tell.

Perhaps he found a scent:
A rabbit. Off he went.
He'll come back home all spent.

Groundhogs, they say, can fight;
And raccoons will at night.
He'd not know one by sight!

I've called and called his name.
I'll never be the same.
I blame myself . . . I blame . . .

All *he* knows is the park;
And now it's growing dark.
A bark? *You hear a bark?*

The Villanelle

(*pronounced* villa-knéll)

I say: Look up this queer word *villanelle:*
A form that has five tercets, one quatrain.
But how which lines repeat, now, who can tell?

I'm sure that you could write one very well;
So never mind what no one will explain.
I say: Look up this queer word *villanelle.*

I think of longer words too hard to spell:
So villanelle should cause you little pain.
But how which lines repeat, now, who can tell?

Just follow me the way you would a bell
And you will need no longer to complain.
I say: Look up this queer word *villanelle.*

Lines one and three in tercet one compel
Attention. Watch for them. Don't ask in vain,
"But how which lines repeat, now, who can tell?"

I leave you with that thought on which to dwell:
Of all these nineteen lines, those two remain.
You can look up this queer word *villanelle;*
And how which lines repeat, now, you can tell.

Turtle

This turtle moved his house across the street.
I met him here about an hour ago.
It is *so* hot, I guess he feels the heat.

Outside, at least, his house looks very neat;
But what goes on inside I do not know.
This turtle moved his house across the street.

No windows, just the four doors for his feet,
Two more for head and tail. Now they don't show.
It *is* so hot, I guess he feels the heat.

He must be tired. I don't know what he'll eat.
Does *he* grow big? Or does his *house* just grow?
This turtle moved his house across the street.

I'll put him near the pond. The grass is sweet.
The dragonflies are fast, but he is slow.
It is so *hot!* I guess he feels the heat.

It's nice to have a house like that, complete
To walk in, float in, sink in mud below.
This turtle moved his house across the street.
It is so hot! I guess he feels the heat.

469

The Ballade

(pronounced bal-ódd*)*

A ballade rhymes with "odd" and it *is* odd, and not
Like a ballad, which tells us a story that tends
Very often toward death. A ballade has a lot
Of surprises, wit, humor; is brief as it blends
This and that. It's a French form, and never offends,
But delights in pure antics. Just eight lines in size
Is each stanza; one rhyme scheme. By rule each one
        ends
In refrain, like "Beefburgers served only with fries."

A ballade has three stanzas: the prominent spot
Is line eight in each one — the refrain — which
        extends
Your idea, be it silly, or trite, or just rot;
And it's on this eighth line that your topic depends.
Now let's see what our beefburger business com-
        mends.
It appears we can't buy them *alone*. No one tries
To, I guess. I hate fried things! What fool recom-
        mends
A refrain like "Beefburgers sold only with fries"?

I'm that fool. I just *chose* it. I thought I knew what
Would sound pleasant: beefburgers *and* fries are old
        friends.

Most Americans eat them. French fries, when they're
    hot
And quite crisp, aren't too bad; but the vender who
    vends
Them — what right has he got to dictate? No one
    spends
Extra money for what one dislikes! If you're wise,
You will *not* write ballades when some rascal defends
And refrains like "Beefburgers sold only with fries."

Envoy

Did I mention the *envoy* — four lines? One pretends
There's a prince. So begin it now: Prince, I despise
All fried food. *Ugh!* Those nude little spud dividends!
And refrains like "Beefburgers sold only with fries."

Ballade: An Easy One

Of course I find it fun to write
Ballades. Some people don't, alas!
The best ones gallop swift and light
On anapestic feet.* In class
You'll learn that, like wind over grass,
An anapest goes ta, ta, *tee;*
Or you can say it: trout, trout, *bass.*
It doesn't matter much to me.

In *this* ballade the line is tight
And short and glitters some, like brass:
Iambic — four feet. Let me bite
It oút / for yoú. / As cleár / as gláss,
We're not deep down in some morass
Of verse; we're sailing smooth and free.
If our next rhyme is *sassafras,*
It doesn't matter much to me.

And yet it *should* because, in spite
Of all your skill, you must amass
A lot of rhyme words — *sprite, might, kite —*
And juicy ones like this — *crevasse;*

* Which is the meter of the preceding ballade.

472

And you can feel now, as I pass
From *class* to *grass* to *bass,* I see
The end in sight. But I am crass:
It doesn't matter much to me.

Envoy
Prince, am I finished? Lad or lass,
Ballades may run *you* up a tree.
If my balloon is filled with gas,
It doesn't matter much to me.

The Clerihew

(pronounced clérry-hue)

1

The clerihew
Is a tricky form for you.
The first two lines state a fact;
The second two, how you react.

2

Perhaps a name,
Then a line describing the same.
You take off from there.
What you say is your own affair.

3

Samson, you might say,
Had long hair for his day.
What horrid thoughts we harbor
For the first lady barber!

4

Or think of the planet Mars
All covered with scars,
Canals, and ice caps too;
Not the likes of me and you.

5

Babe Ruth
Is a legend now to youth.
I saw the Babe in action,
Which was a greater satisfaction.

6

The Nottaway
Never got away
To the Platte away
Out thataway.

7

The skunk
Has a lot of spunk.
If the reason isn't plain,
He will gladly explain.

8

Cheyenne
Is sheer magic; but then
So is Broken Bow,
Moosejaw, and Jump-off Joe.

9

You can see the opening line
In these clerihews of mine
Can be long or short. But the zip
In the short *is the crack of a whip*.

10

The dolphin's brain
Is something we would fain
Know a lot more about.
Not so the brain of a trout.

11

When a rooster crows
Everybody knows
The dawn made him do it.
That's all there is to it.

The Cinquain

(*pronounced* sin-cáne)

1

This is
The form of the
Cinquain. The five lines have
2, 4, 6, 8, 2 syllables
As here.

2

Be/gin
That's two/Two more
Now/six/syl/la/bles/and
Then/eight/syl/la/bles/You/count/them
Now/two

3

No/rhymes
All/so/eas/y
Just/keep/count/cor/rect/ly
I'm/di/vid/ing/the/syl/la/bles
For/you

4

Let's build
Something. Guess what?
A cellar first. A floor.
A ceiling. A roof over it.
A house.

5
Four paws,
four feet, head, tail,
two eyes, two ears, a mouth,
a good nose for smelling things. *What?*
A dog.

6
Pen, ink,
table, paper,
an idea, a first line,
more lines, changes, great long pauses,
A poem.

7
Puzzle
chemical too
Get a dictionary
Hexamethylenetetramine*
Got it?

8
Plant seed
Water it well
Sprout divides   just two leaves
Days pass   weeks   months pass   It grows up
Maybe

* *Héxsa-méthill-een-tétra-mean*

478

9
Two wheels
Handlebars   seat
Two pedals   chain   a brake
Two tires   One of them is flat now
Fix it

10
Behind
Always behind
Following after me
In the way   but still my little
Brother

11
Everything
Small   very small
Neat   orderly   lifelike
Real as the real thing   only small
Doll's house

12
A sound
Far off   haunting
You must listen quite close
Else you won't hear it faintly roar
Seashell

13
Tough words
Doubling letters
Where you don't expect them
Desiccate and *obbligato*
C B

14
Who sees
The redwoods for
The first time won't forget
Their tallness ageless look saying
Always

15
Do you
Care for crickets?
I love their summer sound
Late fall I like one in a house
Chirping

16
What lives
Under water
Very fierce Eats small fish
Then crawls on land to shed its skin
And fly?

17
Love all
Rivers   They are
Man's friend   ally   power
Near them he builds his cities   Keep
Them clean

18
Try your
Hand at cinquains.
They *show* their form, teach you
To be simple, direct, precise.
Are you?

Haiku

(pronounced high-coo)

1
Because it is short,
Japanese three-line haiku
Almost writes itself.

2
Count the syllables!
Five each in lines one and three,
Seven in line two.

3
Syllable writing,
Counting out your seventeen,
Doesn't produce poem.

4
Good haiku need thought:
One simple statement followed
By poet's comment.

5
Take the butterfly:
Nature works to produce him.
Why doesn't he last?

6

Man invents the wheel.
For centuries it runs well.
Today it runs him.

7

Mackerel-shaped cloud
Means a hard rain very soon.
Mackerel will swim.

8

The whistler buoy
Keeps his lips wet in the fog
Quite far from Kansas.

9

Wind, surf, low tide, fat
Horse. Small girl wears her new spurs.
Gulls fly. Her hat flies.

10

All these skyscrapers!
What will man do about them
When they have to go?

11

The bolas spider
Weights a short thread-end with goo,
Twirls it, catching bugs.

12

The town dump is white
With seagulls, like butterflies
Over a garden.

13

The big truck says, *No!*
Little VW says,
I'll pass! Yes, I *will!*

14

In the Laundromat
Dryer the Angels always
Seem to beat the Sox.

15

Wind ripples the grass,
Waves rock the boat, but clouds have
To drag their shadows.

Subject Index

487

488

489

Index of First Lines

493

494